Advance Praise for *Unhitched*

"Oona Metz's *Unhitched* is exactly the guide women facing divorce need. Metz shares the wisdom she's earned over years of practice as a therapist, as well as practical feedback for the confusing, and often gut-wrenching season of life that accompanies a divorce. For any reader who seeks advice, reassurance she is not alone, and comforting guidance during the lonely road to divorce, Oona Metz's book is a must-read."

—Christie Tate, *New York Times* bestselling author of *GROUP*

"*Unhitched* is a compassionate guide and steady hand for any woman facing the upheaval of divorce, whether chosen or not. With equal parts empathy and practicality, Oona Metz offers the emotional support you need to weather this grief-filled transition, along with clear, tactical steps to navigate the messy in-between."

—Melissa Urban, *New York Times* bestselling author, *The Book of Boundaries*

"With wisdom, heart, and refreshing honesty, *Unhitched* feels like a trusted companion through one of life's hardest passages; a gift for anyone facing the end of a relationship—not only providing validation and comfort but also empowering readers with the tools to rebuild their lives with strength and hope."

—Wendy T. Behary, LCSW, author of *Disarming the Narcissist*

"*Unhitched* isn't just a guide, it's a companion. Whether you're still deciding whether to leave, figuring out how to co-parent without losing your mind, or rebuilding your sense of self after it all falls apart, this book meets you exactly where you are. Metz speaks directly to the emotional reality of this transition in a way that makes you feel seen. . . . It's the book every woman navigating divorce deserves."

—Olivia Howell, Cofounder and CEO of Fresh Starts Registry

"The information and exercises in *Unhitched* make it a compass in a time of great upheaval. The warmth and empathy provide an emotional anchor as Oona Metz lovingly guides readers to turn divorce turmoil into self-transformation."

—Marisa Franco, PhD, *New York Times* bestselling author of *Platonic*

"In *Unhitched*, Oona Metz has gathered wisdom gained from her decades of work into a highly accessible, emotionally relatable, and practical guide. Throughout the book, beautifully designed exercises deepen the reader's experience, clarify personal obstacles, and highlight pathways to transformation and growth."

—Patricia L. Papernow, EdD, author of
Surviving and Thriving in Stepfamily Relationships

"*Unhitched* is a compassionate and clear-eyed guide that every divorcing woman deserves. Practical and affirming, it is written with a true inclusivity that embraces LGBTQ+ relationships as fully as any other. Oona Metz offers not just a roadmap but a steady hand to hold along the way."

—Dawn Dais, author of *The Sh!t No One Tells You About Divorce*

"*Unhitched* is the must-read guide for any woman navigating the pain of separation or divorce. Blending compassionate advice, practical exercises, and fascinating real-life vignettes, the book gives you the tools and encouragement you need to heal, grow and move confidently into your next chapter."

—Vikki Stark, MSW, author of *Runaway Husbands*

"Few books prepare therapists for the terrain of divorce as effectively as *Unhitched*. Oona Metz offers a steady and compassionate presence, guiding readers through the turmoil of separation and showing women not only how to endure the climb but how to emerge stronger, clearer, and renewed. […] For clinicians, Metz provides a trusted framework for guiding clients through one of life's most difficult transitions. This book will quickly become an indispensable companion on the journey of healing and renewal."

—Lorraine Wodiska, PhD, CGP, President, American Group Psychotherapy Association

"*Unhitched* is the compassionate, clear-eyed guide divorcing women need. Oona Metz brings the deep experience of a therapist and the warmth of a trusted friend. Her message is clear: your life isn't ending, it's just beginning."

—Reshma Saujani, founder of Girls Who Code and Moms First, host of *My So-Called Midlife*

Unhitched

The Essential Divorce Guide for Women

Oona Metz

GALLERY BOOKS
New York   Amsterdam/Antwerp   London
Toronto   Sydney/Melbourne   New Delhi

G

Gallery Books
An Imprint of Simon & Schuster, LLC
1230 Avenue of the Americas
New York, NY 10020

For more than 100 years, Simon & Schuster has championed authors and the stories they create. By respecting the copyright of an author's intellectual property, you enable Simon & Schuster and the author to continue publishing exceptional books for years to come. We thank you for supporting the author's copyright by purchasing an authorized edition of this book.

No amount of this book may be reproduced or stored in any format, nor may it be uploaded to any website, database, language-learning model, or other repository, retrieval, or artificial intelligence system without express permission. All rights reserved. Inquiries may be directed to Simon & Schuster, 1230 Avenue of the Americas, New York, NY 10020 or *permissions@simonandschuster.com*.

Copyright © 2026 by Oona Metz

All rights reserved, including the right to reproduce this book or portions thereof in any form whatsoever. For information, address Gallery Books Subsidiary Rights Department, 1230 Avenue of the Americas, New York, NY 10020.

First Gallery Books trade paperback edition January 2026

GALLERY BOOKS and colophon are registered trademarks of Simon & Schuster, LLC

Simon & Schuster strongly believes in freedom of expression and stands against censorship in all its forms. For more information, visit BooksBelong.com.

For information about special discounts for bulk purchases, please contact Simon & Schuster Special Sales at 1-866-506-1949 or *business@simonandschuster.com*.

The Simon & Schuster Speakers Bureau can bring authors to your live event. For more information or to book an event, contact the Simon & Schuster Speakers Bureau at 1-866-248-3049 or visit our website at *www.simonspeakers.com*.

Interior design by Karla Schweer

Manufactured in the United States of America

10 9 8 7 6 5 4 3 2 1

Library of Congress Control Number is available.
ISBN 978-1-6680-7538-8
ISBN 978-1-6680-7540-1 (ebook)

 Let's stay in touch! Scan here to get book recommendations, exclusive offers, and more delivered to your inbox.

To all the brave women+ who have trusted me with their stories

Contents

Introduction ... 1

Part One
Chart Your Route ... 17

1. Getting Oriented ... 19

    The Three Ways a Divorce Begins ... 19

    When You Initiate the Divorce ... 23

    Most Common Reasons Women Initiate Divorce ... 24

    Telling Your Spouse Your Marriage Is Over ... 31

    When Your Spouse Initiates the Divorce ... 33

    Traumatic Divorces ... 37

    When Your Divorce Is Mutual ... 43

Cynthia's Story ... 47
A Passive Husband and Parenting Differences

    Can You Relate? ... 50

2. Preparing for Your Journey — 55

    Develop a Support System — 55

    Create a Self-Care Plan — 59

    Gather Legal Information — 61

    Decide on a Legal Path — 63

    Organize Your Finances — 67

    Practice Meeting Your Own Needs — 68

    Think About Your Children's Needs — 71

Margaret's Story — 77
Infertility and Conflict with In-Laws

    Can You Relate? — 81

3. Following the Map — 85

    The Five Phases of Divorce Grief — 86

    How Long Does It Take to Get Divorced? — 91

    Will You Ever Get Over Your Divorce? — 92

Mandy's Story — 94
Infidelity, Narcissism, Gaslighting, and Love Bombing

    Can You Relate? — 98

4. Sharing Your Location — 105

    Who, What, and When to Tell About Your Divorce — 105

    Telling Your Children — 106

The Five Elements of a Divorce Conversation
with Children   109

Telling Your Friends, Family, and Colleagues   116

Other Ways of Sharing the News   122

Part Two
Climb the Mountain   127

5. Staying on the Trail   129

Feeling All the Feels   130

Grieving the Loss of the Marriage   148

Hidden Losses   150

6. Hitting Your Stride   161

Six Steps to Processing Your Emotions   163

Three Simple Ways to Soothe Yourself   166

The Power of Positive Affirmations   168

Moving Too Quickly or Too Slowly?
Find the Right Pace   170

What Does Progress Look Like?   176

Permission to Do Less   177

Jada's Story   180
Alcoholism and Living in Limbo

Can You Relate?   183

7. Preparing Children for the Journey Ahead — 187

- What the Research Says — 188
- What This Means for Your Children — 189
- The Five Phases of Divorce Grief for Children — 190
- Support Strategies from Infancy to Adulthood — 194
- What Children Need — 198
- Six Tips for Co-Parenting with an Uncooperative Ex — 202
- When the "Best Interest of the Child" Is Not in Your Best Interest — 204

8. Finding Shelter: Transitioning from One House to Two — 209

- Nesting Pros and Cons — 210
- Choosing a Parenting Plan That Works for Everyone — 214
- Shared Parenting Time Templates — 215
- Creating a Smoother Transition Day — 225
- Sharing the Pets — 231

Part Three
Recharge, Refresh, Refocus — 235

9. Renegotiating Your Boundaries — 237

- Three Steps to Make Clear Boundaries — 242
- New Boundaries with Your Ex — 243
- The BIFF Approach: Brief, Informative, Friendly, Firm — 248
- New Boundaries with Your Friends and Family — 252
- New Boundaries with Your Children — 255

Martina's Story — 259
Coercive Control, Financial Abuse, and Intimate Partner Violence

- Can You Relate? — 263

Part Four
Reach the Summit — 271

10. Finding New Partners or Flying Solo — 273

- Dating Again — 273
- Four Reasons to Wait Before You Date — 279
- A Whole New Dating World — 281
- Casual Sex, Relationship, or Marriage? — 282
- Keep Yourself Safe — 285
- Five Biggest Dating Mistakes After Divorce — 286
- Ready, Set, Date! — 292
- Trusting Again — 294

11. Enjoying the View — 297

Stronger at the Broken Places — 298
Post-Traumatic Growth — 300
Reflect on Who You Want to Be — 302
Five Things to Let Go Of — 305
Five Ways to Let Go — 307
Forgiveness — 310
Apologies — 313
Giving Back — 314
Ten Practical Things to Do After Your Divorce Is Finalized — 316

Resources — 319
Acknowledgments — 327
Endnotes — 329

Author's Note

The vignettes in this book do not correspond to any actual persons, living or dead. All the people described here are composites of the thousands of stories I have heard in my practice. Details have been changed to protect the privacy and confidentiality of my clients.

While some of the ideas and exercises you find here may be therapeutic, *Unhitched* is meant to be a source of support and information rather than a substitute for professional treatment. Many people find they need therapeutic support during their divorce. I have included a list of mental health services in the Resources section on page 319.

Language is both powerful and imperfect. In writing this book, I wanted to use language that reflects the full range of experiences while remaining clear and accessible. The term "woman" is not meant to exclude but to encompass. While I use the term "woman" for simplicity, this book is meant to be inclusive of anyone who identifies as female or nonbinary.

Introduction

"How is it possible that nearly half of marriages end in divorce and I don't know a single person going through one?" I hear this question all the time from women in my practice. In large part, it's why I decided to write this book. *We need to talk about divorce.*

I am a psychotherapist who specializes in helping women navigate the emotional impacts of divorce. I've worked with hundreds of women, and the vast majority have left my office stronger, happier, and more confident than when they entered. Just as every marriage is unique, every divorce is as well. However, many divorces follow a similar trajectory, and most of the feelings women experience during that process are universal.

As children, many of us dreamed of getting married when we grew up. None of us dreamed of getting divorced. *That was never part of the plan.* But here you are, and now you need to get through your divorce and emerge with strength, clarity, and confidence. You can do it. This book will help.

While you read these pages, I hope you'll find solace knowing you're not alone, your feelings are valid, and you will be okay in the end.

Maybe you'll even go from believing the end of your marriage was the worst possible outcome to believing it offers benefits and opportunities to become a stronger, more empowered version of yourself. For many women, divorce results in growth and transformation they never imagined possible.

Divorce has both a legal and an emotional arc. The legal aspects of your divorce will typically have a clear beginning, middle, and end. There are plenty of books that describe the legal and financial aspects in detail. (See Resources at the end of the book for a comprehensive guide.)

The emotional arc of divorce, on the other hand, tends to be more complicated. For many women, the emotional aspects begin long before the first call to a divorce attorney and extend far beyond the final court date. Unlike most books on divorce that focus on the legal or financial implications of divorce, *Unhitched* will guide you through the *emotional* side of divorce, from the earliest days of anguish and confusion all the way to healing and empowerment. You'll find actionable advice, relatable stories, and reflective exercises along the way that will help you feel less isolated, more confident, and better informed.

Your personal journey has begun. There's no going back to who you were before your divorce, only onward to a new you. The good news is you don't have to do it alone. Treat this book like a trusted friend, one who will walk beside you all the way from heartbreak to moving on to your new life.

My Personal Story

I have a lot of experience with divorce, both personally and professionally. My parents divorced when I was six years old, and I spent my childhood going back and forth between their homes. Many members of my extended family are divorced, including grandparents, aunts, and uncles. And I've been divorced twice.

Many years ago, my first marriage ended after my wife and I had been together for ten years and married for five. Our daughter was two years old when we made the painful decision to move into separate homes. Just three weeks after my ex moved out, my best friend died of breast cancer. That year was the hardest of my life. Grieving my closest friend at the same time my marriage was ending was at times unbearable. I had difficulty parsing my feelings, and I feared my pain would remain at a fever pitch forever. I worried all the time—about my finances, about the impact on my daughter, and about being alone. As a solo parent, I felt overwhelmed by responsibilities, and yet my heart ached for my daughter when we were apart.

A few things kept me afloat that first year. I had a cheerful, energetic toddler, wonderful friends, and a thriving therapy practice. When I was married, my life felt whole, but during my divorce, I compartmentalized my time into parenting, working, and grieving. When I was in parenting mode, I kept busy caring for a child who would not let me sleep in, forget to eat, or be too serious. When I was at work, I felt useful and relieved to be focused on my clients' problems rather than my own. Anytime I wasn't parenting or working, I grieved. Some days I cried; some days I got angry. There were days when it was hard to eat and nights when sleep was elusive.

Even though I didn't miss the dynamic with my ex that eventually led to our divorce, I missed being married and part of an intact family. At forty-one, I was much too young to lose a friend to breast cancer and, in my eyes, too young to be getting divorced. I longed to talk to other women who could relate to my experience, but it was hard to find them.

The second year post-divorce was far better than the first. My grief became more manageable. My irregular yoga practice became more regular. I began to enjoy, rather than dread, my non-parenting time. My friends and family showed up for me, and my anger toward my ex slowly dissipated. I started to understand that divorce was not a static process but a transformative one. I began to see that my co-parenting relationship with my ex could evolve as well.

While at first heartbreaking, the divorce dissolved the parts of our dynamic that didn't work and created space for a co-parenting relationship that did. It wasn't an evolution I wanted or expected. Yet, in the end, it turned out to be the best outcome for me and for our family.

My relationship with my ex has gone through many iterations. When we first divorced, I had trouble letting go of the hope she could become a different kind of person, one more like me. Not surprisingly, this was an issue that carried over from our marriage. With time and distance from our divorce, I recognize how beneficial it is that we have different interests and parenting strengths. We have let go of resentments, we are aligned on our parenting values, and we're friendly when we attend our daughter's events.

Last fall, my ex's sister joined me and my ex at our daughter's soccer game. I was glad to see her, and happy the three of us could sit together on the sidelines. During the game, we chatted and caught up on our respective lives. Afterward, while my daughter got changed, we walked to the parking lot together. Before going our separate ways, my ex's sister opened her arms for a big goodbye hug. I hugged her, genuinely happy to have had the chance to reconnect. She's no longer *my* family, but she will always be part of my daughter's family.

After I hugged her sister, I looked at my ex and she looked at me. It was clear we needed to decide how to say goodbye as well. Even though we saw each other regularly, we had not hugged in the fourteen years since our divorce, and it would have felt awkward to start then. But the pressure was on to do *something*. Without missing a beat, she extended her arm for an elbow bump. Smiling, we elbow-bumped in the parking lot, a compromise that felt friendly yet boundaried, not too close and not too far.

I imagine if this scenario had played out a year or two after our divorce, it would have been tense and awkward. There would have been no elbow bump. But over the years, we have grown into a co-parenting relationship that is cooperative, generous, and flexible. Elbow bumps and all.

Once I got through my first divorce, I was determined never to go through one again. After some time, I felt ready for a new relationship and started dating again. I had grown and changed and was more confident about what I needed in a relationship and what I could give. I had learned important lessons in my first marriage and was ready to put them into practice. Plus, I was a therapist, so I reassured myself I'd be able to spot a compatible relationship a mile away.

Eventually, I met a woman who had a daughter six years older than mine. Our relationship moved quickly, and after a year and a half, we gathered our girls, my cat, and her dog, and became a family. Everyone got along great at first—the pets the only ones not thrilled about sharing the same space. I loved being part of an intact family again, and both our daughters were happy to have a sibling. Just when I thought I had life figured out, our marriage hit stormy weather. Even though I was committed to keeping it afloat, our marital boat took on too much water and ended after only a few years. While the legal proceedings were similar to my first divorce, the way we approached co-parenting afterward was completely different.

Because our marriage was short-term and our girls were already living in two homes when we met, we opted not to burden them with an exponentially more complicated parenting schedule. While couples in first marriages generally share parenting time with their children, parents whose second marriages end in divorce often don't negotiate shared parenting of their stepchildren.

I couldn't bear losing connection with my stepdaughter but knew it wasn't practical to consider a formal co-parenting arrangement in our situation. Committed to staying connected after the divorce, my stepdaughter and I formed our own unique relationship, and I fostered an ongoing sibling relationship between the girls. I know the three of us will always be "chosen family" and remain important to one another. Despite the pain of that marriage ending, I cherish the gift of my stepdaughter and our roles in each other's lives.

My experiences with love, heartbreak, healing, parenting, and stepparenting have informed me personally and professionally. I know I am stronger, wiser, and more compassionate because of them. Like Goldilocks, it's taken me three tries to find the right romantic fit, but I'm now in a long-term, loving relationship with a supportive partner.

My Professional Story

I've been a therapist in private practice near Boston, Massachusetts, for over thirty years, specializing in group therapy and treating women navigating divorce.

Many years ago, when I got divorced the first time, I was desperate to talk to other women who shared my experiences. I tried to find a support group, but sadly no such group existed. I relied on other kinds of support, but a seed was planted in my mind. A few years later, I started a Divorce Support Group for Women+. Therapists, attorneys, and mediators were happy to have a place to refer their clients, and the group filled quickly. As word spread among divorce professionals and the women who attended, the referrals poured in and I started two more groups. Since then, hundreds of women have participated, and all three groups continue to this day.

Eventually, the waitlist for my groups got so long that I decided to develop a training program to teach mental health professionals how to lead them, and now there are similar groups running not only in Boston but across the country as well.

The purpose of these weekly groups is to provide emotional and interpersonal support for women navigating divorce. Group members are in pain when they arrive—feeling scared, sad, confused, angry, and often guilty. The group offers a welcome space to talk, cry, gain perspective, and develop coping strategies. Although the groups address painful topics, both crying and laughter are frequent and cathartic. Bonds form quickly and easily across race, income, and sexuality differences as members connect over their emotional experiences. They report feeling safe and understood, heard and seen—all fundamental building blocks of healing.

At the beginning, many members share similar concerns:

> **What do I do with this flood of feelings?**
>
> **Will I ever feel whole again?**
>
> **How can I support my kids?**
>
> **How will I manage alone?**
>
> **Will I ever find someone else to love?**
>
> **Will I ever get over this?**

The women who attend my groups are hungry for practical information and stories of other women who've gone through divorce and come out the other side. They want to learn from books, podcasts, and movies that mirror their experiences. Most importantly, they want to learn from real people just like them. While the shame and stigma of divorce has decreased over the years, we still don't have enough spaces for authentic, vulnerable discussions about the emotional impact of divorce. Celebrities often whitewash their experiences ("We are divorcing with the utmost kindness and respect"), which can inhibit real conversations about difficult topics.

Two years ago, when I started writing *Unhitched*, there were no recent divorce books for women written by therapists. The only book I had to recommend to my clients was published over two decades ago and in need of an updated revision. I couldn't quite believe the scarcity of content given the immense need, but a thorough search yielded nothing. Standing atop a mountain after a long hike in celebration of a friend's birthday, I declared I wanted to write the book that my group members need, that all women going through divorce need. I pulled out my laptop the very next day.

I've heard thousands of stories about divorce from hundreds of women over the years. They're the inspiration for the vignettes compiled in this book. Many of the people in these stories share aspects of real group members' experiences, but to protect privacy, all names, identifying information, and circumstances have been changed. I hope you'll see yourself in these vignettes, if not in the specifics of each one, then in the feelings so many women experience as they navigate this journey.

Who Is This Book For?

I have written this book for anyone who identifies as a woman navigating divorce, but the information may be helpful to people of all genders. My Divorce Support Groups for Women+ include nonbinary people, and their experiences and insights are woven into this book as well. Women who aren't legally married but are experiencing the breakup of a romantic relationship will also see themselves reflected here.

This book is for you if you have children or are child-free. (Chapters 7 and 8 are solely focused on children, and there is information on parenting throughout). You may be on the younger side, having been married for only a few years, or you may be a grandmother wondering how to talk to your adult children about divorce. You may be earning a high income, getting by paycheck to paycheck, or without any income of your own. You may be the one to initiate the divorce, or your spouse may have decided for you. This book will offer you insights whether you are contemplating divorce, have already begun, or have finalized the legalities.

While there are special considerations for LGBTQ+ people going through divorce, the common threads of emotions, coping techniques, and personal transformations outweigh most differences sexuality might present. Over the years, many LGBTQ+ people have joined my support groups and have found them just as valuable as straight women do. The vignettes you'll read here include women who are navigating divorce with men as well as women navigating divorce with other women. No matter the gender of your spouse, you'll find commonalities in the stories.

Many women think about getting divorced for years before making the decision. For some of you, this book may be the very first step long before you decide to act. Gathering information and support will help you feel more prepared and empowered as you navigate the road ahead. I hope you'll find the information useful, the vignettes relatable, and the exercises thought-provoking.

Are the Experiences of Marriage and Divorce Really That Different for Men and Women?

Yes! In the United States, societal norms around gender and heterosexual marriage continue to have an enormous impact on how we structure relationships and family life. The benefits of heterosexual marriage are often unevenly distributed between men and women, especially after the couple has children. While women have worked toward equality in many realms, significant gender inequality persists in income, parenting, and caring for the home.

Recent research from the US Bureau of Labor Statistics shows that women in heterosexual marriages spend more time than men caring for children at every stage. When children are under six, women spend more than twice as much time physically caring for children and four times as much time providing educational activities. When children reach school age, women spend three times longer than men organizing educational activities and nearly twice as much time transporting children to school and activities. Women also read and talk to their children more than three times as much as men.

According to a study from the University of Michigan, the average heterosexual woman in the US ends up with seven more hours of housework per week when she gets married while men end up with one less hour per week.

Research shows that marriage benefits men more than women, especially in the areas of health, wealth, and well-being. This may be part of the reason heterosexual men are less likely to initiate divorce—marriage works better for them. When it comes to divorce, men are more likely to isolate themselves from friends and family, avoid the grieving process, and jump into work or a new relationship right away.

In fact, I've often heard divorce professionals say, "Women grieve and men replace."

Women tend to be more actively engaged than men in initiating, maintaining, *and* ending marriages. In the US, heterosexual women initiate 69 percent of divorces. Are women less invested in marriage or less committed? Actually, quite the opposite. Many of the women who attend my support groups value the institution of marriage but left their spouses because they couldn't find an alternative. In many of those marriages, their spouses had disengaged or abandoned the spoken and unspoken rules of marriage, leaving them backed into a corner with divorce as their only viable option. Often, after years of trying to improve their marriages without success, these women were also the ones who had to bear the work of calling an end to them.

Many women face a decrease in income and an increase in child-rearing responsibilities when they divorce. The good news is women tend to fare better than men psychologically after divorce and *often report feeling happier out of the marriage than in it*. This may be because they tend to be more comfortable seeking emotional support and have wider social supports. Women are often active participants in their own recovery and are accustomed to creative problem-solving, skills that help with major life transitions.

What do all of these statistics mean for you? It's likely you have been working hard—at work and at home. If you're a parent, you work extra hard taking care of your kids. I bet you are tired. Maybe even exhausted. I'm guessing you have carried the weight of your relationship and your family. You make the social arrangements, call the plumber, remember the birthdays, schedule the dentist appointments. You've done the bulk of the work to keep your family going.

If you're navigating a divorce, chances are the work you do to keep your house and family humming is underappreciated by your spouse. If so, you are in good company. Many women contemplating divorce feel their spouse is more like an additional child in the house than an adult partner. In fact, data from the Bureau of Labor Statistics has shown that in heterosexual marriages, mothers spend *more* time doing household chores and *less* time sleeping than their divorced counterparts. This is the case even when women outearn their husbands.

How to Use This Book

Feel free to read this book from start to finish or jump around from one chapter to the next. Take notes in the margins or underline the things you want to return to. Pick it up at different stages of your divorce and put it down when you need a break.

You'll find short, easy-to-read sections, as I have learned from countless women in the throes of divorce that the ability to read dense texts goes out the window. This is normal. Don't worry! Your ability to read whole books will return. In the meantime, this book offers bite-sized chunks of useful information you can process, retain, and apply. I hope you'll come back to this book several times, over several years, to reread at different stages.

Along with practical information you can use immediately, you'll get to read five longer stories of women at the end of their marriages. As a society, we still don't talk about divorce freely and authentically enough. Many women going through divorce feel isolated and worry that no one will understand their experience. The stories here are composites of real situations and real people I've seen in my practice but presented in a way that no one person is identifiable. Any resemblance to real people or events is unintentional and purely coincidental.

Each story addresses a different marital theme, and whether you have faced that particular issue or not, you are bound to find aspects you relate to. Even though your marriage and divorce are unique, you will inevitably see parts of yourself in these stories. I hope reading about the experiences of other women will help you feel less alone. After each story, you'll have an opportunity to consider how you connect to the themes and then reflect on your own experience.

You'll also find reflective exercises sprinkled throughout the book. You can take notes in your journal or in these pages, or just think about them in your head. It's okay to skip any or all of them.

At the end of the book, you'll find helpful resources, including Ten Practical Things to Do After Your Divorce Is Finalized, and information about mental health services, online support groups, financial and legal assistance, recommended reading, podcasts, and more.

Your Divorce Journey

I've divided this book into four parts and used the metaphor of climbing a mountain because for many women, that is what divorce feels like. You need a good map and the right supplies at the beginning to get you oriented to where you are going and how you will get there. The trail to the top will have rocky terrain and stormy weather, and you will be challenged to the core as you face obstacles and adversity at every turn. But if you take one step at a time, you'll reach the top, where you'll gain new perspective as you emerge with more courage and clarity than you imagined possible. The challenge of climbing that mountain will always be part of your story, as will the resilience and freedom that come when you reach the summit.

Chart Your Route

This section includes the beginning of your divorce—how it all starts. In Chapter 1, we'll lay out the three different ways divorce begins—you initiate, your spouse initiates, or you come to the decision together. Then, in the first of five longer stories throughout the book, we'll meet Cynthia, who decides to divorce due to her husband's passivity, chronic underemployment, and parenting differences. Chapter 2 will outline concrete ways to get prepared legally and financially, and will help you develop a support system. We'll meet Margaret, whose marriage to her wife was marked by stress from fertility treatments and a lack of support from her in-laws. In Chapter 3, we'll explore the Five Phases of Divorce Grief and the kinds of hidden losses you may experience. You'll meet Mandy, whose story includes infidelity, narcissism, betrayal, and gaslighting. Finally, in Chapter 4, we'll review how and what to tell your children, friends, and family about your divorce.

Climb the Mountain

This section is all about navigating the emotional rollercoaster of divorce. In Chapter 5, we'll discuss the feelings of anger, sadness, fear, and guilt that accompany divorce, as well as feelings of relief. Chapter 6 includes strategies and exercises you can use right away to help you cope with the all the emotional ups and downs. Then you'll meet Jada, who divorces her husband due to his alcoholism. Chapter 7 focuses on what your children need to weather the storm of divorce, and Chapter 8 includes parenting plan templates and practical advice about how to make transition day less stressful.

Recharge, Refresh, Refocus

Once you've survived the emotional rollercoaster of divorce, we'll turn toward opportunities to build a new life and identity on the other side. In Chapter 9, we'll talk about renegotiating boundaries with your ex, your kids, your family, and your friends. You'll also meet Martina, whose divorce includes elements of coercive control, financial abuse, and intimate partner violence.

Reach the Summit

While every divorce is painful, you *will* get through it, maybe even as a stronger, more resilient version of yourself. In Chapter 10, we'll talk about dating—first yourself, and then other people. You'll find lots of exercises to help you figure out what you need to make good relationship choices. Chapter 11 focuses on reflection, owning your new identity, gratitude, forgiveness, and moving forward. Finally, you'll find an extensive list of resources, including websites, books, and podcasts.

Divorce is about endings, grief, and loss, but it's also about beginning something new. Divorce is not a failure. Instead, it's a restructuring of a family into a healthier constellation and an opportunity to reflect on who you are and who you want to become. Ultimately, I hope this book will give you the tools to move through the emotional journey of divorce with confidence and self-compassion. I have helped hundreds of women do it. I have done it myself. And I know you can do it, too.

Part One

Chart Your Route

1

Getting Oriented

Let's start by acknowledging that, even if the divorce was your idea, this is not where you hoped you'd be. You don't want to be part of the Divorce Club—no one does, even though it has a lot of great members and offers valuable benefits. I know it's hard to believe now, but over time, you will meet wonderful divorced friends and come to appreciate some of the advantages of divorce. In the meantime, let's dive into learning more about how divorce begins.

The Three Ways a Divorce Begins

Regardless of who introduced the idea of ending the marriage, getting oriented to the journey of divorce will help prepare you for what comes next. There are a few ways a divorce begins. Each one leaves a unique emotional footprint. In this chapter, we will discuss each of the following scenarios:

- When you initiate the divorce
- When your spouse initiates the divorce
- When you and your spouse make a mutual decision to divorce

Regardless of how they begin, all divorces involve loss, grief, and pain. Popular culture may lead us to believe mutual-decision divorces are "easy," or that the person who initiates a divorce experiences less pain, but I believe there's no such thing as a painless divorce. No matter which camp you're in, you'll need to think carefully about the financial, legal, and emotional implications of your next steps. You will probably never feel 100 percent ready. Still, it's important to be as prepared as possible for what comes next.

The good news is that women in *all three categories* have the potential to transform their divorce into an opportunity for self-reflection, growth, and empowerment. The majority of women I see in my practice are devastated when they arrive—fearful, sad, angry, and overwhelmed. But by the time their divorce is finalized, many end up feeling grateful that their marriage ended, *including the women who didn't initiate their divorces*.

Of course, not everyone ends up happier post-divorce. Some women experience additional challenges that leave fewer resources for healing. For instance, many women faced with severe financial consequences after divorce must prioritize their basic needs over opportunities for growth. While most women find workable co-parenting arrangements, for some, post-divorce parenting battles can result in a perpetual state of high stress. Just as every physical ailment needs time to heal, the wounds of divorce also need a chance to mend without getting reinjured by ongoing conflict.

Women who don't attend to their own growth, don't reach out for support, or hold on to old resentments have a much harder time healing. Given the road ahead, it's more important than ever to prioritize asking for help and getting the care you need. Your decision to read this book already proves you're ahead of the game by being open to growth and support.

Sylvia and Cara—A Tale of Two Sisters

Growing up, Sylvia and Cara had a loving relationship. Despite living on opposite coasts as adults, they remained close. They each married and divorced around the same time, but their experiences differed drastically.

Sylvia and her husband, Rick, had a friendly but emotionally distant marriage. They got divorced when Rick came out as gay. Sylvia had a great group of friends and was already in individual therapy when her divorce began. She loved knitting, hiking, and fishing, and was an active member of a local political group. She had suffered from anxiety since childhood but had sought help and developed good coping strategies. Rick's coming out was upsetting for her, but they were able to remain relatively amicable. Sylvia and Rick had no children and similar incomes, making their financial and legal settlement proceed quickly and efficiently.

Cara, on the other hand, was married to Ernest, an alcoholic who refused to seek help. They struggled for years with his addiction and its impact on their marriage and three children. Cara worried about the kids' safety around Ernest. She also worried about finances, as he was chronically underemployed. Ashamed of Ernest's drinking, Cara isolated herself from her friends and neighbors. After filing for divorce, she was reluctant to ask for support, and she couldn't afford a therapist. One day, trying to be helpful, Sylvia asked if Cara had any hobbies to help her cope with stress. "Hobbies? Sylvia, I have three children and no money. I don't have time for hobbies," Cara snapped.

Cara's divorce proceeded slowly and was full of unexpected twists and turns. Ernest wanted joint custody of the kids, but he was often intoxicated around them. He hired and fired two attorneys and then decided to represent himself. Cara often felt overcome with rage, sorrow, and frustration, all while working and parenting her three children.

Sylvia and Cara had very different divorce journeys. Sylvia felt guilty that her divorce seemed easier to navigate, and she worried about her sister. Cara's divorce was chaotic and stressful, and at times, she worried it would never end. She suffered from anxiety and depression as her divorce dragged on for two years. Cara initially resented Sylvia's broad support network and self-care strategies, but eventually realized she needed more support, too. She joined an Al-Anon group, and by year three, when her divorce was finalized, she finally began to experience some relief. Although their stressors and coping strategies differed, both Sylvia and Cara ended up happier in the end.

As this story shows, there are many factors that determine how a divorce will proceed. While Sylvia was heartbroken, she had good support, finely tuned coping skills, and a cooperative spouse. Cara's divorce, on the other hand, involved many more stressors. Cara had less support and fewer coping strategies. As a result, her divorce had a greater emotional impact. While some things related to your divorce will be outside your control, the coping strategies and supports you develop can make a huge difference.

When You Initiate the Divorce

No matter the circumstances, ending a marriage is heart-wrenching. While it may ultimately be the healthiest decision, it is never easy or simple. If you are initiating divorce, chances are your marriage has been in trouble for quite some time, and you are feeling the fallout. You are probably worried about yourself, your kids, and your future. Many women who initiate divorce worry about the impact on their spouse as well. You may also be feeling tremendous guilt and shame about your decision. Certainly, this was not the plan when you got married.

Before making the final decision to divorce, ask yourself if you've done everything possible to save your marriage. You may have taken these steps already, but if not, be sure your spouse knows just how challenging the marriage has become for you. It's important that you share your thoughts on how you can both work to make it better. Then do as much as you can to make meaningful changes. Some steps might include marriage counseling, individual therapy for you and/or your spouse, pastoral counseling, parent coaching, or participation in a 12-step program. This way, either your marriage will improve, or you will know you did all you could before ending it.

The exception to this is in cases of physical, sexual, or emotional abuse. Abuse is not a relationship issue—it's a safety issue. Abuse is a pattern of power and control, not a mutual dynamic that can be resolved through improved communication. If you are initiating divorce because of abuse, be sure you have a safety plan in place before you leave.

Knowing you did everything in your power to save your marriage will help you feel less regret, guilt, and shame as you move forward. And sometimes making the changes actually works, allowing you to stay in a fulfilling marriage.

Most Common Reasons Women Initiate Divorce

You may have been considering a separation or divorce for many years now. Or maybe you've recently learned something that has permanently broken your trust in your spouse. In the past, divorce professionals referenced three main reasons people divorce—addiction, abuse, and adultery—but today we know there are many reasons women initiate divorce, including:

- A marriage that is too hot—too much fighting, tension, and toxic conflict

- A marriage that is too cold—not enough communication, tenderness, or intimacy; one or both partners are shut down

- Sexual, emotional, or financial infidelity—this includes romantic affairs, emotional affairs, and financial abuse, misuse, or deception

- Physical, emotional, or sexual abuse—insults, assaults, aggression; a pattern of power and control

- Coercive control—a pattern of intimidating, humiliating, controlling behavior

- A spouse who has long periods of unemployment or underemployment

- A spouse who is extremely passive

- A spouse who weaponizes their incompetence (intentionally acts as if they are unable to do certain tasks, creating more work for their partner)

- Ongoing conflicts in parenting styles, especially when there is a negative impact on the children

- A spouse's untreated addiction to alcohol, drugs, sex, gambling, pornography, or technology

- A spouse's untreated mental health issues

- An inability to manage anger appropriately

- A sexual mismatch or lack of intimacy altogether

- Realizations about sexuality or gender that are incompatible with the marriage

- A significant difference in values or lifestyle

Maybe you relate to one or more of the reasons above or have your own motivations. Whether your reasons are crystal clear or more ambiguous—you are allowed to divorce. Your needs matter and you are allowed to act on them.

> *Forgive yourself for not knowing what you didn't know before you learned it.*
>
> **Maya Angelou**

Because women are socialized to be responsible, empathetic, and attuned to others' needs, deciding to leave can result in feelings of guilt and shame. If you are carrying guilt, it might be helpful to consider who *left* the marriage and who is *ending* it. Sixty-nine percent of heterosexual divorces are initiated by women, but that doesn't mean women aren't invested in the institutions of marriage and family. Rather, women are often more active in all stages of marriage—starting, maintaining, and ending them. When faced with an uncooperative spouse who can't or won't work on the marriage, many women feel they have no choice but to end a marriage that's already over.

Jackson and Claire—Backed into a Corner

Jackson was a college professor, and Claire worked in finance. After twenty-three years of marriage and two kids, Claire learned Jackson had been having an affair with one of his graduate students for the past six years. This student babysat for them and even came to Thanksgiving one year. Claire was shocked when she found out. She spent weeks raging at Jackson, unable to eat, sleep, or get out of bed. She couldn't trust Jackson anymore, but even worse, she felt she could no longer trust herself. After all, she thought she knew her husband inside and out. Jackson apologized profusely and promised he would end the affair immediately. They contacted a marriage counselor and scheduled emergency sessions. Very slowly, over time, they were able to repair the rift in their marriage. Jackson took responsibility for the pain he had caused, and they both owned up to the ways they had not attended to the marriage.

Two years after Claire discovered the affair, the couple went away together to celebrate their twenty-fifth wedding anniversary. Claire felt as if they had finally reconnected, and their marriage was even stronger than before the affair. When Jackson went for a swim in the hotel pool, he left his phone on his chair. Claire saw a text come in that made her heart start to pound. Jackson was still having an affair with the graduate student. Claire began sweating and thought she might faint. Her head swirling, she ran from the pool, unsure what to do next. Claire later learned Jackson had never ended his affair, and she realized she couldn't trust him ever again. Although she had been hopeful their marriage was back on track, she couldn't bear this second betrayal. With a heavy heart, she decided to file for divorce.

Claire wanted to stay married, but believed she had no choice but to end things. While Claire initially felt guilty, her therapist helped her understand that even though she had filed for divorce, *it was Jackson who had left the marriage.* She noted how hard Claire had worked to repair the initial betrayal as well as the marital issues. By the time Claire learned Jackson's affair was ongoing, she'd already put two years of hard work into their marriage, believing Jackson was working on it, too. Though her decision to divorce might have seemed abrupt to outsiders, Claire knew she'd done everything in her power to rebuild her marriage. She recognized she would never be able to trust Jackson again if they stayed together.

Accepting your reality and letting go of hope

It can be hard to accept the reality that your marriage and/or your spouse is not going to change. You've invested time and energy into this relationship and don't want to give up now. Maybe you keep thinking that once life settles down, or you get that new job, or the kids are more independent, then things will get better.

The sunk-cost fallacy is a concept that refers to staying in a situation because of the time and effort you've invested in the past, even when that situation no longer serves you. Often people remain in unhappy marriages simply because they've been together for so long. Many women worry ending a marriage means the time they invested in it was wasted. But your marriage was not a waste—it served a purpose, even if only for a period of time. Gaining awareness of this fallacy can be empowering. You may come to realize that investing in something that no longer works isn't worth it. Ultimately, the energy you spent in the past should not dictate decisions about your future.

In order for things to improve, *both members of a couple need to agree on the problem and commit to fixing it.* Making meaningful change becomes nearly impossible when only one person is doing the work. There is a significant difference between marriages where both spouses are actively working to improve versus those where only one person (or neither person) is making changes. If you've identified what needs to change and your spouse doesn't agree, or refuses to work on it, you'll either need to accept the status quo or end your marriage. It's important to believe people when they tell you, both in words and actions, that they cannot or will not change.

In an unhealthy marriage, one of the hardest things to give up is the hope it will get better. This is especially true if you are an optimistic person, a can-do fixer who is used to solving your own problems. If your marriage has had ups and downs, with some years better than others, it may be even more challenging to give up hope. Whether your spouse is a decent person who simply cannot meet your needs or someone who has been abusive, you may be tempted to linger in your marriage, hoping your spouse will finally change. You're the only one who can make the very personal decision about how long you're willing to wait for things to get better.

> Accepting the reality of your situation and letting go of the hope that your marriage will improve is a painful but important step.

Coming to terms with the end of your marriage

You may feel extremely stressed and saddened as you come to terms with the level of dysfunction in your marriage and the knowledge that it's not going to change. It may be hard to admit things have gotten this bad. Wrestling with these emotions can impact you both emotionally and physically. You may have trouble sleeping, or feel shaky or nauseous. Some women feel depressed or anxious at this stage. Your brain may keep cycling through the same thoughts again and again. It may be difficult to concentrate or be fully present.

Being in an unhealthy marriage has likely added additional strain to your life. You may be so used to the tension, conflict, and stress that you no longer realize how much extra weight you are carrying. While being in a familiar and unhealthy relationship is sometimes more comfortable and convenient than the unknown, it's *not necessarily better*. There is life after divorce, and you do have the power to become happier and healthier.

True self-care is not salt baths and chocolate cake, it is making the choice to build a life you don't need to regularly escape from.

Brianna Wiest

Telling Your Spouse Your Marriage Is Over

Make sure you feel certain you want to proceed with divorce before you talk to your spouse. Bringing up the idea of divorce when you are not certain may result in your spouse unilaterally proceeding with divorce as a defensive move. Once you're ready to tell your spouse you want to end the marriage, keep these things in mind:

- **Assess your safety.** If you are in an abusive relationship, or your spouse has ever been violent or volatile, make sure you have a safety plan. This may involve telling your spouse in front of another trusted person or having a safe place to go immediately after you break the news. Leaving is often the most dangerous time for women in abusive relationships.

- **Choose the right time and place.** There will never be a perfect moment to bring up divorce, but certain times are better than others. Have the conversation in a private setting and avoid high-stress times. If you have children, make sure they can't hear your conversation.

- **Be calm and kind.** Try to avoid announcing your intention to divorce in the middle of an argument or in a reactive way. Instead, approach the conversation when you feel calm. Be caring, honest, and compassionate while still upholding your needs. How you tell your spouse you want a divorce can set the tone for the legal proceedings ahead. "I know this may come as a surprise, but I have done a lot of thinking, and I'd like to get a divorce" is going to be more effective than lashing out in the middle of an argument, "That's it! I'm done! It's over, get out!"

- **Keep the focus on what you need rather than what your spouse has done.** If you create a list of what your spouse has done wrong, you invite argument. Instead, talk about yourself and your needs. Your spouse can't argue with your feelings (though they may try). "I'm lonely in our marriage, and I don't feel like my emotional and physical needs are being met" is more effective than "You never talk to me, you're never affectionate, you clearly don't care about me."

- **Be firm.** Stand firm on your resolve. Don't try to convince your spouse this is a good idea or something you're doing to make their life better. You will likely receive pushback, but try to avoid getting into an argument about your decision. You are not asking for permission; you are stating your intention. It may be helpful to say, "I know this isn't what you want, but it is what I want." Getting married takes two willing partners, but getting divorced only takes one.

- **Be prepared for an emotional response.** Your spouse will likely have an emotional reaction to your news. Don't try to talk them out of their feelings or attempt to negotiate in this heightened emotional state. This is not the time to figure out finances, parenting plans, or living arrangements. That comes later. You may want to give your spouse space, and saying something like "I can see how angry and upset you are. I am going to take a walk while you calm down and we can return to this later" may give you both a needed break after you have delivered your news.

- **Use your powers of prediction.** You know your spouse better than anyone and will likely be able to predict how they are going to react. Plan in advance for this.

- **Plan for afterward.** This conversation will likely be highly emotional and stressful. Make sure you have a plan for yourself when the conversation ends. Meeting up with a friend or having an appointment with your therapist to debrief your conversation will help you to process whatever you are feeling.

Telling your spouse your marriage is over is a big step. We will discuss how to prepare yourself emotionally, legally, and financially in Chapter 3. For guidance on how to tell your children or other people about your divorce, see Chapter 4.

When Your Spouse Initiates the Divorce

If you are the one who is being left, you are likely experiencing a wide range of feelings. Hopefully, you and your spouse discussed the ways your marriage was in trouble before you were told it's over. But if you found out abruptly with no warning, you may feel as if the rug has been pulled out from under you. Some people describe feeling like their spouse has ignited a bomb in their living room. You may be in a state of shock or feel numb at first. It's not uncommon to experience fear at this stage, as your future has suddenly become so uncertain. This was *definitely not the plan*, and you are probably reeling.

As you process this new information, you may feel:

- angry or rageful
- betrayed
- abandoned
- rejected

- sad or devastated

- confused and fearful

- ashamed or guilty

- lonely

- exhausted

- numb

At times, you might experience contradictory feelings. For instance, you may feel angry at your spouse for leaving in one moment and devastated or ashamed the next. These kinds of varying emotional states are perfectly normal. Your emotions might fluctuate minute by minute or week to week. I can assure you these intense emotional whirlwinds won't last forever, even if it feels that way right now. They will decrease in frequency and intensity over time, and we'll discuss actionable ways to process your emotions in upcoming chapters. For now, know your feelings are normal and valid. Many other women have felt just like you do right now.

Your feelings aren't right or wrong, good or bad, and none of them are permanent. You don't need to apologize for having them.

Self-care is a must

In the days and weeks after your spouse announces they're leaving, it's especially important to take good care of yourself. You may find it hard to sleep, eat, or concentrate. Bouts of crying and episodes of rage are normal at this stage. If your spouse has been planning an exit for a long time, they may come across as cold, unfeeling, or distant. It might make you feel crazy to see how little your spouse is reacting when your own emotions are so intense, but remember, they have been thinking about this and playing it out in their mind for a while now. You've just gotten this information and have had little to no time to process it.

> *Caring for myself is not self-indulgence.*
> *It is self-preservation.*
>
> **Audre Lorde**

During this time, treat yourself as gently as you can. If you had the flu or broke your arm, you would be taking good care of yourself. Yet many people still believe they should be able to muscle through emotional pain. If your job allows it, take a sick day or a sick week. Eat comfort food. Find a way to sleep. Seek professional help from your doctor, therapist, spiritual leader, acupuncturist, and/or massage therapist rather than suffering alone. Reach out and begin building the vital support network you will need for what is coming next.

Exercise: A One-Minute Somatic Release

Unpleasant emotions linked to traumatic experiences can impact your central nervous system. A somatic release helps regulate it by tapping into the body's natural capacity for healing.

This is a great exercise to practice when you feel overwhelmed or stressed. Try to do this exercise several times a day. Pay attention to how you feel before and after you do it.

- Unclench your jaw.

- Drop your shoulders.

- Shake out your hands.

- Move your eyes side to side.

- Stick out your tongue as far as you can.

- Take three deep belly breaths.

- Repeat.

Remember that your body will reflect your emotional pain back to you. It may be hard to pay attention to your mind, but at least listen to your body by giving it the care it deserves. If you can only do two things for yourself, focus on eating every day and sleeping every night. Lack of sleep will make everything worse, so don't delay in getting help if your mind is racing so much at night that you can't fall asleep or stay asleep. If more natural remedies like sleep meditations or herbal supplements are not working, ask your doctor about over-the-counter or prescription medications. In the following chapters, I will talk more about a variety of ways you can support yourself.

Traumatic Divorces

Marriages that end abruptly, without any warning, can be traumatic. Trauma is a response to a deeply distressing event that overwhelms an individual's ability to cope and leads to feelings of helplessness. In most cases, traumatic responses are not permanent and fade with time and/or treatment. Trauma diminishes one's sense of self and can cause unpredictable emotions, flashbacks, and physical symptoms.

A traumatic event is one that **fundamentally changes the way you see the world.** We all have certain belief systems about how the world works, including how marriage works. An abrupt and unilateral ending can challenge your belief system about your marriage *and* your spouse. You may question other fundamental beliefs as well, *including about yourself.* Even if you consider yourself an emotionally stable person, a sudden end to the marriage may still rock you to your core. This level of trauma can impact you regardless of your intelligence, social connections, or mental health. You might find yourself wondering for the first time:

- Was our entire marriage a lie?

- Did I fool myself into thinking we had a happy marriage?

- Am I a good judge of character? Can anyone be trusted?

- Can I trust myself to know how people close to me are feeling?

- Am I unlovable?

These are common reactions to many kinds of betrayals, and while these questions may feel overwhelming at first, they will arise less frequently and with less intensity over time.

"But I thought we were happy"

It's important to know that your spouse may present a wildly different narrative of your marriage at this juncture. It can be destabilizing to hear them say they have not loved you or been happy for years if this doesn't match your experience. Keep in mind that your spouse may feel the need to justify their decision to leave by exaggerating their negative views about your marriage. It's likely that your story and your spouse's story will differ, and that both of them will change over time. For right now, trust your own narrative. As hard as it may be, try to give up controlling your spouse's narrative.

Sonya and Christopher—A Traumatic Ending

Sonya and Christopher were married for forty years. They had three young adult children and were planning to buy a second home when Christopher had a massive heart attack. Over the next six months, Sonya took him to all his appointments and helped him with his rehabilitation. Once he was well enough, Christopher started running daily and got into the best shape of his life.

On the one-year anniversary of his heart attack, Christopher came back from a long run and announced to Sonya that he had been unhappy for years and wanted a divorce. She was completely shocked. There had been no indication that he was unhappy. In fact, they were planning a trip to Spain in just a few months. Sonya pleaded with Christopher to go to couples therapy with her and not rush the decision, but Christopher was resolute and moved out of their house a week later.

Sonya fell into a deep depression. She felt like Christopher had blown up their life. She spent much of the following year just trying to survive each day. She woke up crying at night and slept too much during the day. She had no appetite and lost a lot of weight. Once an avid reader, Sonya found she lacked the concentration to enjoy books. She was miserable, and she was also furious at Christopher. Sometimes she called him at night and screamed at him for ruining her life. But in addition to feeling angry and sad, Sonya missed Christopher. She missed the life they had and the life they were planning. After all, he had been a great partner right up until the end. She felt ashamed that she missed him, and conflicted because her friends and family all encouraged her to hate him. Her shame made her feel even lonelier. Sonya was trapped in a downward spiral.

Eventually, she realized she needed help and found a support group for women going through divorce. She discovered she

> could relate to other group members' feelings, even when their stories differed from her own. She opened up quickly when she recognized the other members were not there to judge her. To her surprise, when she described how much she still missed her husband despite being angry with him, she saw women around the circle nodding in agreement. The group reassured Sonya that they, too, had been in her position, carrying a multitude of feelings at once.

Christopher's abrupt and unilateral decision was traumatic for Sonya. It challenged her beliefs about her marriage, her husband, and, ultimately, herself. Sonya was overwhelmed with questions about what had happened and why Christopher had decided to leave her. His actions left her reeling. Individual therapy helped her understand the parts of her marriage that weren't working, and to accept she would never know the whole story from Christopher's perspective. Eventually, she was able to develop her own narrative of their marriage and let go of the hope Christopher would share his as well. This allowed Sonya to move on with her life and regain a sense of control.

Exercise: **Core Beliefs and Positive Attributes**

Check the box next to the core beliefs you had about your marriage and/or your spouse when your marriage was going well, before divorce became a possibility. These should be beliefs you relied upon to structure your worldview. You can add any additional core beliefs you had as well.

- ☐ My marriage will last "until death do us part."

- ☐ I will know if our marriage is in trouble, and we will be able to make it better.

- ☐ I can trust my spouse. My spouse would never lie to me.

- ☐ My spouse is a fundamentally good person who would never intentionally hurt me.

- ☐ If I have health problems when I get older, my spouse will be there for me. We are looking forward to retirement together.

After making your check marks, circle the statements you can no longer rely on. If you circle several of them, it's likely the end of your marriage has been traumatic.

Now write down five positive attributes about yourself. Don't skip this part of the exercise. This is important.

Here are a few examples to get you started.

- I am strong.

- I have been through hard things and survived.

- I am a good parent.

- I am a good friend.

- I am smart.

- I am good at solving problems.

1. _____
   _____
   _____

2. _____
   _____
   _____

3. _____
   _____
   _____

4. _____
   _____
   _____

5. _____
   _____
   _____

Now, next to each attribute, write down an example from your past that demonstrates that strength. Here are a few ideas:

- I am strong. Even though my parents were abusive, I persevered and made a good life for my kids.

- I have been through hard things and survived. I lost my job and had a terrible car accident in the same year, but I survived.

- I am a good parent. My kids are happy and have strong friendships.

- I am a good friend. I am often the first person my friends call to help them solve a problem.

- I am smart. I figured out how to fix the dryer when it broke, which saved me hundreds of dollars in repair costs.

- I am good at solving problems. When my mother suddenly needed assisted living, I figured out a way to get her the care she needed.

Acknowledging these positive qualities will help in all areas of your life, including your divorce. While navigating your divorce, keep this list handy as a reminder of your strengths.

When Your Divorce Is Mutual

Some divorces are mutually agreed upon by both partners. While this kind of divorce doesn't involve the pain of one person being left, it still often includes feelings of loss, disappointment, and regret. Divorce represents the end of a shared life together. Navigating all the accompanying emotions can be exhausting. Even when the decision is mutual, it only comes after a period of conflict, tension, or mismatch in the marriage. It's not unusual for both members of a couple to feel deep sadness as they come to their decision.

Letting go of the social benefits of marriage can also be destabilizing, even if both people agree it's the best option. Family and friends may weigh in or take sides in ways that are intrusive or unhelpful. People often want to place blame on one party and may have difficulty accepting that the divorce was truly mutual.

Children and family members will have their own reactions. Parents who mutually decide to divorce still have to develop and execute thoughtful, child-centered parenting plans, a process that is often complex and emotionally fraught. Disagreements about parenting plans can gnaw at the couple's original goodwill toward each other and complicate the divorce proceedings.

In addition, some people have difficulty adjusting to living alone. Especially for people who have been married a long time, making the transition from being part of a couple to being single is a significant identity shift. Finding new social supports and adjusting to a new schedule takes time and energy.

Elaine and Charmaine—A Mutual-Decision Divorce

Elaine and Charmaine met when they were both eighteen and got married right after high school. Each of them had grown up in households that were chaotic and unpredictable, and they were eager to make a stable home for themselves. They worked hard in their twenties and bought a house. Elaine found a good job at a bank and joined a hockey league. Charmaine worked in the service industry for a few years but was eager to see the world beyond her hometown. Eventually, she got a job with an airline and was gone for several days each week. Elaine missed Charmaine when she was working and pleaded with her to go back to waitressing in their small town. Meanwhile, Charmaine felt she had finally found the career of her dreams, one that allowed her to see different parts of the country. As the years went by, Elaine became lonelier and more resentful of Charmaine's career path. When Charmaine was home, she experienced Elaine as angry and withdrawn. Elaine wanted to start a family, but Charmaine wasn't ready for that step.

When Charmaine was offered a promotion to fly the international routes, she was racked with guilt. She was thrilled at the prospect but knew this would be heartbreaking for Elaine. She accepted the promotion and called a marriage counselor the very next day. After six months of counseling, the couple came to a place of acceptance that they no longer wanted the same things out of life. Charmaine was able to stop blaming Elaine for holding her back, and Elaine was able to see that Charmaine's career choices were not meant as a rejection. They used marriage counseling as a place to grieve their life together and plan for next steps.

Elaine and Charmaine were headed toward a messy and caustic divorce before they sought professional help. Their marriage counselor helped them understand that staying together would require too much sacrifice for both of them. Their dreams were no longer compatible. They worked to let go of blame and understand it was their innate differences that kept them in conflict. By the time they reached the legal and financial aspects of the divorce, they had resolved much of their anger and resentment, which allowed the process to run smoothly. Although their mutually decided divorce involved loss and the pain of letting go, the outcome was beneficial for both of them.

In a mutually decided divorce, the financial, legal, and emotional aspects may be easier to navigate, but that is not always the case. Sometimes when both parties agree on ending their marriage, they still disagree about how to divide finances, who gets to stay in the home, and how to structure parenting plans for their children. Although your decision may be mutual, you will likely experience feelings of grief and loss as your divorce marks the end of an important chapter.

Cynthia's Story

"Feeling like the only adult in the relationship was lonely and frustrating."

Sam and I grew up in really different types of families, which was appealing at first. He went to private school, I went to public school. His family was upper class, and mine was working class. I'm the oldest of four girls and was responsible for my younger sisters while my parents worked. Sam is an only child and grew up with a lot of money. His father traveled for work and his mom doted on him—he was their golden child. I realize now how our different upbringings affected our marriage.

When we met during our sophomore year in college, I loved everything about Sam and his family. He grew up in a big house by the ocean, and his mother spoiled us whenever we visited. Being part of their family made me feel special. We got to travel and eat in fancy restaurants—things I never did with my own family. I loved that Sam was spontaneous and up for any kind of adventure. I'm an overly responsible, Type A person, and it was a relief to be with someone who could mellow me out a little.

A year after we graduated from college, we got married. I had always wanted to be a teacher, so I got a job working in a preschool. Sam started a band and worked in a coffee shop so he could focus on his music. Our marriage worked well enough when we were in our twenties. We could afford our rent, I carried our health insurance, Sam's band was playing every weekend, and his parents took us on some really nice vacations. Life was good.

I wasn't worried because I figured eventually he would grow up and get a real job.

Things changed for us when Sam's band got invited on a five-week tour in Europe. They wouldn't be making much money, but he felt it was an amazing opportunity. He quit his coffee shop job after saying he couldn't let his bandmates down. I was worried about our finances, but he was so excited. Despite wanting to support him, I also felt resentful. When he came home after the tour, he didn't seem to appreciate that I was working and paying all our bills. I guess, looking back, that was when our marriage started to fray.

Feeling like the only adult in the relationship was lonely and frustrating.

In hindsight, I realize how much pressure I was under when Sam stopped working at the coffee shop. He hadn't been making that much money, but at least it got him out of bed and gave him a regular paycheck. It meant I wasn't the only one financing our life. Yet despite my nagging, he refused to go back to work.

There were early warning signs, but I just assumed every marriage has its issues.

The year we turned thirty, Sam's parents offered us a gift of a down payment for a house. Since I was the only one working, we needed their help. We bought a cute little house with a huge backyard. When we needed money to make repairs, I begged Sam to find work. He half-heartedly agreed.

I tried to help him with his résumé, but he refused. I forwarded job listings to him, but he wouldn't follow up. When a position opened at my school for a substitute teacher, I offered to talk to my boss. He said he didn't want a job that started that early in the morning.

Every time I tried to help, he refused to let me.

Despite my frustration, I just figured he would land something sooner or later. At least his parents were helping out, but that became complicated, too. There were definitely strings attached to their help.

Eventually, Sam's uncle offered him a job. He worked for a few months but quit because he "felt like a sellout." I began wondering if he might have ADHD. I could see how much medication helped my students with ADHD, but Sam refused to get evaluated. Now I wonder if things would have turned out differently if he had gotten diagnosed back then.

I was working full-time, along with doing the grocery shopping, the cooking, and most of the cleaning.

I'd come home from work and find Sam napping on the couch. He was still playing in the band but not doing much else. I tried to keep my anger under control, but every few weeks, I would just lose it on him. For a few days, he would help around the house, and I became hopeful things were going to change. Then the pattern would repeat. Although I was fed up, I also still loved him and wanted to start a family.

Somehow, I naively thought having kids would force him to grow up.

When our son was born, everything went from bad to worse. Sam still didn't have a job, so I went back to work and he took care of our baby. It was a disaster. I would come home to music blaring so loudly he couldn't hear our son crying. I quickly realized we were in real trouble and I needed to get out. It was hard enough he couldn't care for me, but it was unacceptable that he couldn't care for our son.

Sam didn't want to get divorced—he had a good deal being married to someone who did everything for him. But he also didn't want to work on the marriage. He wouldn't get a job and he clearly couldn't be trusted to do the childcare. I felt like I had no choice but to divorce him. I never wanted a divorce—I wanted to be married with lots of kids and a white picket fence—but I had to face reality.

One of the hardest things to let go of was the hope that our marriage would get better.

Getting divorced was one of the hardest things I've ever done, but it was also the right decision for me and my son. Sam is well into his thirties and still being supported by his parents. His band never had any real success. He sees our son on Sundays, and they have a good relationship, but I am still the one who does all the parenting. At least now I'm just parenting one child instead of parenting Sam, too.

Can You Relate?

Just like every marriage is unique, every divorce is as well. Yet many of the circumstances and feelings that arise from divorce are similar. Seeing yourself in others' stories can help you feel less alone. Put a check mark next to the sentences you relate to.

- ☐ I wasn't worried because I figured eventually my spouse would grow up and get a real job.

- ☐ Feeling like the only adult in the relationship was lonely and frustrating.

- ☐ There were early warning signs, but I just assumed every marriage has its issues.

- ☐ Every time I tried to help, my spouse refused to let me.

- ☐ I was working full-time, along with doing the grocery shopping, the cooking, and most of the cleaning.

- [ ] **Somehow, I naively thought having kids would force my spouse to grow up.**

- [ ] **One of the hardest things to let go of was the hope that our marriage would get better.**

> ### *Oona's Notes*
>
> - Differences in childhood family dynamics between spouses can significantly influence the marital relationship.
>
> - Many marriages work when the couple is in their twenties but then break down as responsibilities increase over time.
>
> - Relational patterns established early on in a marriage become more difficult to change the longer they persist.
>
> - It's often difficult for women to leave marriages that aren't working because they are invested in the concept of marriage and want to keep their family intact.
>
> - In most marriages, couples agree early on about how they will share financial, parenting, and home responsibilities. If one spouse refuses to do their part, yet objects to a divorce, it can leave the remaining partner feeling backed into a corner.

Exercise: **Early Warning Signs**

Many women look back at their marriage and wonder if there were warning signs all along, or if something changed. Reflecting on the dynamics of your marriage is an important step toward growth and healing. This can also help you avoid unhealthy patterns in future relationships. As you reflect, remember to be compassionate with yourself. If you ignored warning signs or didn't see red flags at all, you are not alone.

Looking back now, what were three early warning signs in your marriage? Try to be as specific as possible.

1. _____
   _____
   _____

2. _____
   _____
   _____

3. _____
   _____
   _____

Women stay in dysfunctional marriages for many reasons, including:

- Financial considerations
- An optimistic outlook on life, including the hope that a spouse will change
- The belief that all marriages are hard and take work
- Worry about the impact of divorce on kids
- The fear of being alone
- Not wanting to repeat their parents' messy divorce

Many women can identify warning signs in hindsight, though for some, there were none. Perhaps you thought you had a happy enough marriage and were blindsided by your spouse's unilateral decision to divorce. At first, you may feel shocked as you reflect on what you perceived to be a great marriage. I encourage you to bookmark this page and come back here in a year's time. Women who initially believe they had wonderful marriages often realize over time that there were cracks in the foundation. Taking time to reflect on the strengths and challenges in your marriage, now and in the future, can yield valuable insights.

2

Preparing for Your Journey

You're on your way toward a divorce. The path ahead will be bumpy, full of twists and turns, and probably will take longer than you hope. Some things on this journey will be beyond your control. However, there are a number of things you *can* do to help yourself feel more supported. Being proactive now, in the early stages of divorce, will pay off in the future, paving the way to less distress and greater empowerment. If you were going on a long hike up a tall mountain, I know you'd pack all the right supplies. Think of your divorce as a long trek, too. Let's talk about what you'll need along the way.

Develop a Support System

You may already be talking to close friends or family members about the difficulties in your marriage. If not, once you know you are going to separate or divorce, it's important to tell a trusted friend or family member that your marriage is ending. You will need the support of friends and family on this journey. Many women keep their marital conflicts private due to loyalty, shame, or a reluctance to hear feedback. However, when you feel ready, getting support is a crucial step.

Most people have strong reactions to divorce, and their responses are often impacted by their own values, marital situation, or religious beliefs. For example, your aunt who has been happily married for fifty years may urge you to stay married because she did, despite all the conflict in her marriage. Or your unhappily married college friend may encourage you to get divorced so you can test the waters and pave the way for her. You will likely receive a lot of advice at this stage, and some of it may not be helpful. I encourage you to tell a few trusted people, especially the ones you think will put their own judgments aside. Because their reactions may be biased, hold on to the advice that's useful and discard the rest. For more on who, what, and when to tell, see Chapter 4.

In addition to talking to friends or family members, it can be beneficial to speak with a therapist. You are embarking on a major life transition that will bring up a lot of feelings. Having a supportive, neutral person to talk with each week can be a vital part of your self-care plan. Choose a therapist who has professional experience working with women going through divorce. Make sure to ask them if they have any moral or religious objections to divorce before you start working with them. You'll want to see a therapist who can help you decide what is right for *you*.

Joining a divorce support group can help you feel less alone and give you a community of people who understand how you feel. Although nearly half of marriages end in divorce, many of the women in my support groups struggled to find women going through the same experience. Divorce is often an isolating process, and having people you can talk to *who really get it* will help you feel less alone. In a support group, people will be at different stages of divorce. Those who are further along in the process offer hope to the people just starting out that they, too, will get to the other side.

Try to get a personal recommendation for a therapist or support group. If you need further resources, check out the Psychology Today website or other therapy-finder sites. You can also ask your attorney or mediator for resources. Some churches and synagogues offer groups as well, though most are not run by therapists. See the Resources section at the end of the book for more mental health resources.

If you don't have access to a therapist or support group, you can join a social media group for women going through divorce. These allow you to post anonymously or just read about other people's experiences. Decreasing your sense of isolation will be immensely valuable. If you do decide to post in a social media group, keep in mind that anything you share could potentially be seen by your ex or used in court. Be sure to keep your posts anonymous.

Identify your teammates

Having a team to guide you through a divorce is crucial. In addition to hiring a lawyer and/or a mediator, a financial planner, and a therapist, you'll want to think about your important unpaid consultants: your friends and family. It is too much for one person to take on all your emotional needs related to your divorce, so be sure to recruit multiple people to help.

Here are some of the supports you may find helpful:

- A good, nonjudgmental listener whom you can call just to vent

- A cheerleader—someone who will send you uplifting texts and cute animal videos

- A practical friend—the one who knows how to fix your printer or can help you develop a budget

- An activity partner—your exercise, shopping, or movie buddy

- A new emergency contact person—this is important if you don't want your ex called in an emergency

- A parent friend—someone who can pick your kids up from school or activities in a pinch

---

Exercise: **My Support Team**

In each column, write down a few names of friends or family who fit each description. Some friends might fit in more than one category.

These people will become your divorce team. You do not have to do this alone, nor should you. Don't forget to thank them for being there for you and ask how they're doing every once in a while. It's okay for your relationship to be a little lopsided at this time, but remember that your friends and family members have their own stresses and challenges, too.

Good Listener	Cheerleader	Practical Friend
_____	_____	_____
_____	_____	_____
_____	_____	_____
_____	_____	_____

Activity Partner	Emergency Contact	Parent Friend
_____	_____	_____
_____	_____	_____
_____	_____	_____
_____	_____	_____

Create a Self-Care Plan

I cannot emphasize enough the importance of practicing self-care. Women often feel depleted in unhealthy marriages, like they are running on fumes. Divorce is stressful, takes a long time, and won't run on your timeline. You'll be impacted both physically and emotionally. Some women say divorce feels like having to sprint through an entire marathon.

Make sure you're doing your best to exercise, eat right, drink less alcohol and more water, sleep enough, meditate, spend time in nature, and/or take care of yourself in any way you can. You will not be perfect at your self-care activities. There will be some days when you can only do one thing on your list, and others when you can do them all. Try to set realistic goals of little things you can do every day.

In addition to activities that you can fit into your daily schedule, there are other ways to think about self-care. In her book *Real Self-Care: A Transformative Program for Redefining Wellness*, Pooja Lakshmin describes real self-care as consisting of "the internal process of **setting boundaries**, learning to **treat yourself with compassion**, making **choices that bring you closer to yourself**, and **living a life aligned with your values**." While at first glance, you may feel you don't have time or energy for any of that, I can assure you that many of those facets of self-care go hand in hand with healing from divorce. Because you are going through a life transition, you will have choices to make at every junction. The process of divorce actually creates opportunities for a reset in how you live your life. Incorporating Lakshmin's self-care concepts will serve you now and in the future.

For example, you will have the opportunity to **set new boundaries** during your divorce—in fact, it will be a necessity that you can't avoid. In addition to setting new boundaries with your ex, you will probably need to set new boundaries with the other important people in your life as well. We will talk extensively about what boundaries are and ways to set them in Chapter 9.

Throughout this book, I will encourage you to find ways to **nurture self-compassion**. As you come out of an unhealthy marriage, your self-esteem is probably at a low point. Women going through divorce are often hardest on themselves. Some of the exercises throughout the book are designed to help you develop greater self-compassion.

> Self-compassion is one of the most important aspects of self-care. On the days when you can't practice a self-care activity, don't dwell on your shortcomings or blame yourself. Tomorrow is another day to try again.

Divorce will also provide you with plenty of opportunities to make **choices that bring you closer to yourself.** Women are socialized to think about what other people want and need. If you've had an unhappy marriage, I bet you've spent a lot of energy trying to figure out what your spouse and kids need. Divorce is actually an ideal time to shift the focus to yourself, identifying and advocating for what *you* need and want. Ultimately, this is a golden opportunity to live a life that's aligned with your values.

Lakshmin's last facet of self-care is **living a life aligned with your values.** Maybe you already are, but if not, divorce will hand you a chance to do just that. We'll be talking more about your values and intentions in Chapter 11.

Do you see how all the facets of self-care relate to each other? In order to set clear boundaries, you will need to get to know what your needs are and how they align with your values. When you set clear boundaries, you will improve your relationships, and you will find it easier to develop self-compassion.

Gather Legal Information

In addition to developing a self-care plan, you'll need to get acquainted with the legal aspects of divorce. Keep in mind that this may be hard for you as it can feel like a big step, a point of no return. Fear often holds people back from making big changes in their lives. I encourage you to view this as an *information-gathering step* that does not commit you to anything. You don't have to tell anyone, including your spouse, that you're seeking a legal consultation. You don't have to act upon the knowledge that you gain. You are simply educating yourself about the process before deciding how you want to proceed.

Divorce laws are different in each state, so start by researching the laws of the state that will have jurisdiction in your divorce. While this is usually the state where you live, the jurisdiction for your divorce will depend on both spouses' locations and how long each one has lived there. Here are a few questions to get you started:

- Can you file a no-fault divorce? In a no-fault divorce, a couple can end their marriage without either party having to prove wrongdoing.

- Do you live in a state where marital property is equally divided, or in a state where assets are not necessarily divided equally?

- What are the guidelines around child support and spousal support?

- Are there residency requirements? Do you need to live in the state or county for a specified amount of time before you can file for divorce?

- Is there a waiting period for finalizing divorce?

You don't have to hire an attorney and pay a retainer just yet in order to get a few basic questions answered. (A retainer is an up-front payment to an attorney that covers future legal bills; most divorce attorneys require them.) Instead, consider setting up an initial meeting with an experienced family law attorney (or two) who specializes in divorce to get you started. Many attorneys offer initial consultations for free or at a reduced rate. Be sure to ask how assets are typically divided, what factors are considered in determining support awards, and for information on any applicable parenting plans. Many states and family courts provide information about divorce on their websites, and attorneys often have useful information on their websites. Again, each state has different laws about divorce, so make sure your research aligns with the state where your divorce will happen.

Divorce is like any other big decision in your life—you don't have to do it by yourself. If you were having major surgery, you would consult a surgeon to learn more about the surgery and recovery. If you were buying a house, you would consult a real estate agent about where you want to live and what you can afford. A family law attorney can give you a general road map, which will help you make informed decisions moving forward. Just as you wouldn't go to a podiatrist for heart surgery, don't consult a family friend who specializes in real estate law to advise you on your divorce.

Decide on a Legal Path

After researching your state's specific divorce laws, it's time to decide which legal route you would like to pursue. There are several options for you to consider, including mediation, Collaborative Law, and litigation, or some combination thereof. The following is a very brief, general guide. Feel free to use these descriptions as a starting point, but do your own research as well to find the path that fits your unique situation. Before you decide on a legal route, interview a few professionals to determine who will be the best match.

Mediation

Mediation is a confidential process where both parties meet with a neutral third-party mediator who may or may not be an attorney. The mediator cannot legally advise either party but provides information and facilitates communication to help couples reach mutually agreeable financial settlements and parenting agreements. In some states, mediation is required as part of the divorce process. This method is often the most cost-effective, family-friendly, and efficient way to settle a divorce, particularly if both parties are relatively cooperative and have shared goals. While you don't have to hire your own attorney to participate in mediation, consulting with one at regular intervals (especially before you begin mediation and near the end of the process) helps ensure your rights are represented.

Mediation is not the best option in high-conflict cases where one or both parties are uncooperative, dishonest, or abusive. Transparency is vital in mediation, as full disclosure of all financial and other relevant information is required to facilitate a fair agreement. Without transparency and cooperation, the mediation process will break down, resulting in additional costs and delays. If there is a major power differential in your marriage, it may be difficult to advocate for yourself in mediation, and you may feel more supported by having an attorney advocate on your behalf.

In the past, mediation was usually done with both parties and the mediator sitting in the same room. With the advent of online meetings, though, many mediators offer the option to meet via video instead of in person. Online meetings are a great option if you are committed to mediation but find it difficult to be in the same room as your spouse.

If possible, try to get a personal recommendation for a mediator. Otherwise, see the Resources section at the end of the book to find a list of mediation organizations.

Collaborative Law

Collaborative Law is another option for settling your divorce without litigation. In this process, you and your spouse each hire specially trained Collaborative Law attorneys to represent you. Collaborative Law teams often include other professionals as well, such as communication coaches, child/parenting specialists, and financial experts. Their expertise ensures all relevant information is available and understood by both parties, fostering a fair and equitable settlement, along with a plan that works for all family members. Through tools like mediation and negotiation, the team members support the parties as they explore potential solutions to reach a mutually acceptable agreement.

During the Collaborative Law process, all parties agree to work out the divorce settlement without going to court on any contested matter. If an agreement can't be reached, both spouses must hire an alternate legal team to litigate their case in court. This provides extra incentive for the parties to finalize an agreement, because if an agreement is not reached, both parties will essentially need to start the divorce process over with a new legal team, which can be very costly. Similar to mediation, if your divorce is likely to be a high-conflict case, there is a history of abuse, or one party is not cooperating, Collaborative Law may not be your best option.

Litigation

Litigation is expensive, time-consuming, and often antagonistic. Unfortunately, sometimes it's necessary if mediation or Collaborative Law is not going to work. Litigation involves a legal process where you and your spouse resolve your divorce using the family court system. Each party hires attorneys who advocate on their behalf. Not all litigated divorces go to trial; in fact, many are settled before trial begins. Litigation may be your best option if there's a history of marital abuse, or if your spouse is hiding assets or refuses to cooperate in a divorce process. One downside is that a judge may decide the details of your case, which can mean a loss of agency over issues that are important and personal to you. Remember that your legal team ultimately works for you. If they suggest actions that are not aligned with your values or your desired outcome, be sure to speak up and let them know how you'd like to proceed.

People often use more than one legal method to reach a final agreement. Many start with mediation, get stuck, and proceed to Collaborative Law or litigation. On the other hand, some people begin by litigating and end up using mediation or another collaborative process to reach their settlement. Whichever path you use, make sure your legal team has experience with divorce in your jurisdiction.

You know your spouse better than anyone and will be an asset to your legal team as you can predict how your spouse is likely to react.

Organize Your Finances

In addition to getting a legal consultation, you'll need to organize your financial records. One of the first things a mediator or attorney will ask for is financial documentation to get a picture of your individual and shared income and expenses. They will likely ask you to provide your tax returns; the value of your house and car; savings and checking accounts; retirement, pension, and investment accounts; and any high-value personal items like jewelry or art. In addition, they'll need to know your individual and shared debts, including mortgages, car payments, credit card debt, and school loan payments. If you or your spouse own a business, the business will likely have to be appraised for its value.

Gathering all the financial information can be cumbersome and emotionally draining. Tackle it like you would any big project—in smaller chunks that are easier to manage. Decide to spend thirty minutes a day on this project, or invite a friend over for an evening or two to support you. Take your time and go at a pace that feels right for you. If you don't have access to your shared financial documents before beginning the legal process, talk to your legal team about the best way to obtain what you need. All of this can feel overwhelming, so just take the steps you can at this point. It is perfectly reasonable to gather your financial records on your own without your spouse's knowledge, or to collaborate with your spouse if you're in a more amicable situation.

If you have significant or complicated assets, hire a Certified Divorce Financial Analyst (CDFA). A CDFA is a financial expert who is specially trained to help divorcing clients understand the financial implications of their decisions. They will explain all the documents you need to gather and can think creatively with you about how to divide up assets when the time comes. For example, $100,000 in cash versus $100,000 of equity in your home versus $100,000 worth of retirement accounts all have different values and tax implications. These details are important, as the outcome of the divorce will greatly impact your financial future. If you don't own a home or any significant assets, you can skip this step.

Finally, make sure to get a copy of your credit report via one of the three credit reporting agencies (Equifax, Experian, or TransUnion), or call for your free annual credit report at 877-322-8228 (TTY: 1-800-821-7232). Once your divorce is underway, open a credit card in your name only to start building your credit.

Though you may be reeling emotionally right now, getting organized and prepared is crucial. For more financial information and support, check out Gabrielle Clemens's excellent book, *Marriage is About Love, Divorce is About Money*.

Practice Meeting Your Own Needs

You may be used to getting some needs met in your marriage, or, at the very least, *trying* to get them met. However, once you know your marriage is ending, you'll need emotional support from people other than your spouse. This can be challenging, as you may be in the habit of going to your spouse, whether they meet your needs or not. But practice will make it easier. Reach out to the people in your life who love you and can be there for you. Practice doing things on your own. Spend time with friends and family without your spouse. This is a particularly good strategy if you know you are getting divorced but still need to live together for some time.

An extended period of limbo can be especially taxing if you are still living together. Moving into a separate bedroom can be both a practical and symbolic way to increase your sense of independence. If you have this option (many do not) and have children at home, be mindful of the impact on them. With younger children, you may be able to be vague about your move. "Mommy sleeps better in the yellow room" will often suffice. Older children tend to have more questions, as they're more likely to understand that the move has meaning. While I don't advocate lying to older children, sharing your marital issues isn't beneficial either, so again, being vague is best. We'll talk more about how to support and communicate with your children in Chapters 7 and 8.

Shana—Learning to Be Independent

Married for twenty-five years with two kids in high school, Shana and José were more like roommates than spouses. They were sexually incompatible and had not had sex in over a decade. José was a social, talkative extrovert with friends and coworkers, but had become quiet and withdrawn at home. Shana longed to feel more connected to him, but the harder she tried, the more José withdrew. They tried marriage counseling, but José wouldn't open up, so they stopped after a few sessions. Over the years, Shana felt more and more rejected by José and increasingly lonely. When their younger daughter was a senior in high school, Shana decided she would pursue a divorce after their daughter graduated.

Shana joined a support group to help her through this major transition. The group helped her recognize how much she still expected from José. If she had a hard day at work, she wanted to tell him about it but felt disappointed when he was dismissive. When she tried to have a conversation about her daughter, he repeatedly belittled her concerns. Either he claimed he was "busy with work," or he used his favorite line: "I'm sure you'll get over it. It's no big deal." The members of the group helped Shana realize that talking to José was an exercise in futility. Even though she wanted him to respond differently, he had proved that he couldn't or wouldn't. The group encouraged her to use supports other than her husband to get the feedback she needed and deserved. With their encouragement, Shana fixed up a guest room in their house and started sleeping there. She told both José and her daughter that she needed a separate bedroom because he snored so loudly.

At first, she felt guilty, as if she were hiding things from José. But over time, Shana began telling her sister about her ups and downs at work and her best friend about the trials of parenting. She kept José informed about important child-related information but stopped going to him for emotional support. When her computer broke down, she asked her brother for advice instead of José. Within six months, she had made a major shift toward relying on herself, her friends, and family to get her needs met. By the time she told José she wanted a divorce, she had already taken important steps in building her support system and practicing independence.

Shana, like so many women, was only getting crumbs from her spouse. Because she was accustomed to trying to get more from him, hoping to keep the marriage intact, it took time to adjust to seeking support elsewhere. It can be difficult to give up relying upon your spouse, but with practice, you will become more and more independent.

Think About Your Children's Needs

If you're a parent, I know you are worried about the well-being of your children right now. You are most likely feeling some guilt about the impact your divorce will have on your kids. That's a normal and understandable reaction for any parent. This is a good time to think about how you can support your children emotionally, academically, and physically as you navigate next steps. Do they need extra supports or attention in any of these areas? Can you put some of that in place now?

Many parents who are unhappily married decide to stay together because they believe it will benefit their children. The previous research on divorce showed that divorce harmed children. However, much of the current research shows that ongoing marital conflict and tension is more harmful to children than an amicable divorce.

If you and your spouse are constantly arguing or your house is filled with icy silence, staying married will likely negatively impact your children more than a divorce.

It's normal for children to struggle with the transitions involved with divorce. *However, that does not mean they will be damaged.* Most children are incredibly resilient. Although they may initially experience anxiety and grief, most return to their baseline well-being or fare even better after the divorce is settled. There are several ways that you can help them with this transition, which I will outline in Chapters 7 and 8.

Many women have significantly different parenting styles than their spouses. This can create stress for the adults *and* the children. Despite all the gains women have made professionally, most mothers are still responsible for the majority of the childcare. Trying to raise a child with a partner who has significantly different values, strategies, and coping styles can put immense strain on a marriage.

I have worked with many mothers who initiate divorce when their children start mimicking their spouse's worst qualities. These women don't want their children to grow up thinking their marriage is one to be emulated, or that it's acceptable for parents to treat each other poorly.

Fran and Rich—Irreconcilable Parenting Differences

Although their marriage began as a happy one, Fran and Rich had parenting differences that created intolerable conflict. At every turn, Rich criticized or dismissed Fran's parenting decisions. Their twelve-year-old twin boys were often put in the middle and had learned how to manipulate their parents to get what they wanted. Fran hated how strict and punitive Rich was. Rich demanded silence at the dinner table, while Fran wanted to encourage conversation. Rich expected the boys to come home from school and start their homework immediately, while Fran wanted them to have a snack and a break first. During disagreements, Rich criticized Fran in front of the boys: "These boys will never learn manners if you keep letting them off the hook." "Why are you babying them? They don't need a snack before homework." The boys started to criticize Fran in the same way her husband did.

One evening, Fran was watching a movie with the boys when Rich walked in and started yelling that the kitchen was still a mess. Her sons jumped into the fray, angrily asking Fran why she had left the dishes undone. Fran realized how belittled she felt and worried that her children were learning damaging lessons about how marriage works. She could also see they were learning to treat her like her husband did. That night, she called her sister crying, "For years I stayed in my marriage for my children, but now I realize I have to leave my marriage for my children."

Fran tried to make her marriage work for a long time, but Rich became critical and dismissive when they disagreed. Because Rich was rigid and unwilling to compromise, conflicts in their parenting styles eventually impacted every other aspect of their marriage. Fran realized that not only was she suffering, but her kids were as well. Ultimately, leaving Rich became not only a way to save herself, but also a way to protect her sons from the constant arguing and criticism.

You'll find specific information focused on children and divorce throughout this book. Chapter 4 includes a section on telling your children about your divorce. Chapters 7 and 8 are about supporting kids during their journey, from the early days of sharing the news, through adjustments to new parenting schedules and holiday traditions, to nurturing their relationships with both parents.

Exercise: **Packing List**

Make a list of what you've already done to prepare for your separation or divorce, and then a list of what's left to do.

Here are a few ideas to get you started.

- ☐ Identify your support system. Who are the people who can be there for you? Make a list of trustworthy friends, family, and co-workers who you think will be supportive.

- ☐ Make a self-care plan. Start with a list of self-care activities that seem doable. Next, think about when you might schedule them into your week. As divorce is more of a marathon than a sprint, you'll need to plan for things you can keep up long-term. Remember to be patient and compassionate with yourself. If you find it hard to think of your own needs, imagine what you would want for your best friend if she were in your shoes.

- ☐ Gather legal information. Schedule a free consultation with an attorney and/or a mediator.

- ☐ Gather financial information. Print out or take screenshots of any financial records you can access. Obtain a copy of your credit report. Apply for a credit card. Start saving cash in case you are temporarily cut off financially.

- ☐ Practice independence. Plan a trip to see a friend or family member by yourself. Look at your calendar to see when you can go. Brainstorm how you might have more separation in your house. Can you move into a separate bedroom? Spend less time with your spouse. For starters, look at the next week or month. When can you spend time apart?

- ☐ Think about what your children might need. Do they need a therapist or other supports?

Already Done!

☐ _____
☐ _____
☐ _____
☐ _____
☐ _____
☐ _____
☐ _____
☐ _____
☐ _____
☐ _____

To Do!

☐ _____

☐ _____

☐ _____

☐ _____

☐ _____

☐ _____

☐ _____

☐ _____

☐ _____

☐ _____

Margaret's Story

"I kept hoping that once the baby arrived, things would be better."

I met Sofia at work when I was thirty-four and she was thirty-nine. We'd both been in long-term relationships in the past, but this one felt different. We were well matched intellectually and both loved playing sports. We fell in love immediately and moved in together after six months. A year after we met, I proposed. My sisters threw us a bachelorette party, and we had the big gay wedding I had always dreamed of.

My parents loved Sofia and were thrilled about our marriage. Although they were upset when I first came out in college, they eventually came to accept and fully support me. I'm a very social, loud person, whereas Sofia is quieter and likes her alone time. Everyone in my family hoped we would balance each other out.

Sofia's parents are originally from Mexico. They are deeply involved at their Catholic church and very conservative. When she first came out to them, they didn't speak to her for a year. Although they reconciled eventually, there were a lot of hurt feelings that were never talked about. Sofia had a few long-term relationships in her twenties and thirties, but her parents only met one of her partners. Both of her sisters are married to men, and her parents spend every weekend babysitting the grandchildren. They kept their distance with me at first but warmed up over time. That gave me hope they were finally accepting us as a couple.

I was clear with Sofia from the beginning that I wanted to have kids. Sofia felt more ambivalent about starting a family and had no interest in being pregnant. She also worried that if we had children, her parents would favor her sisters' children. Despite her hesitations, she didn't want to deny me the experience of motherhood. We found a fertility clinic, and I began a series of appointments.

Our conflicts around pregnancy began right away. I wanted to talk to my friends about our process while she wanted to keep it all private. I asked her to come to my prenatal appointments, but she didn't want to miss work. When we began choosing a sperm donor, we couldn't agree on the most important criteria. I wanted a donor who was highly educated while she cared more about what he looked like.

Every step of the way she was a reluctant partner. Even though this was *my body* going through difficult hormonal changes and treatments, it was going to be *our child*, and I really wanted her to be involved. Her need for privacy felt too similar to hiding our sexuality from the world. I had done enough hiding of my sexuality as a teenager and I was done with it.

I really needed a partner, but instead, I felt so alone.

I went through four excruciating rounds of fertility treatments without getting pregnant. Each month's negative pregnancy test felt like a new blow. Sofia is a math teacher and much better at numbers than feelings. I tried telling her I felt betrayed by my body, but she couldn't relate.

I felt like I was on an emotional rollercoaster all by myself.

Sofia had asked me to keep our struggles private, but I really needed more support than the crumbs she gave me. I started talking to one of my sisters and my best friend who had both done IVF and could relate. I know it was wrong to go behind Sofia's back, but I was desperate to get the support I needed.

When I worried my body was failing me, the person I needed the most was totally absent.

I was thrilled after I finally got pregnant, but Sofia wouldn't celebrate until I made it through the first trimester. I wasn't willing to hide my excitement, so I told a few friends who I knew would be happy for me. I asked them not to tell Sofia that I had discussed the pregnancy with them.

One Saturday, Sofia and I ran into our friend Denise. She took one look at me and blurted out, "I'm so happy for you guys! Are you having any morning sickness?" I mumbled an answer while Sofia fumed. I was ashamed I had betrayed her but also felt angry that she was squashing my joy. Why couldn't we be excited together? This was supposed to be a happy time. That night, we had our biggest argument yet. I was beginning to see how emotionally shut down she was. She couldn't give me support when times were hard *or* when times were good.

I kept hoping that once the baby arrived, things would be better.

We did get along better for a while, but then we had to tell her family that we were having a baby. Sofia worried they would be disapproving. She had been right to worry. Her parents' first response was to ask how we could bring a child into "this kind of relationship." They were worried about what to tell their friends and priest. Even though I knew how conservative they were, I still couldn't believe they could be this unsupportive. Sofia just sat there silently. It was really awkward. I knew they didn't support gay marriage, but I naively thought they would love our baby. Their reaction was painful, but it hurt even more that Sofia wouldn't stand up to them. She just sat there looking at the floor. I was the one who had to defend our decision to her parents.

I never realized what an impact in-laws could have on a marriage.

When we got home, we had another big argument. Sofia tried to downplay her parents' reaction, and I was furious, not only with her parents, but with her, too. Near the end of the argument, she wondered aloud if her parents were right about it being too hard for our child to have two moms. Something inside me broke at that moment. For me, it wasn't a choice.

Having a baby was so important that I was going to go through with it no matter what.

When she questioned our value as parents just because we were two women, I realized with incredible clarity that I couldn't live like that. That marked the end for me. Although we were compatible in other ways, her lack of emotional intelligence and her unprocessed feelings about her sexuality created too much of a barrier for me.

Even though I was emotionally done, we stayed married for two more years. It was too hard to contemplate leaving when we had an infant. I kept hoping it would get better, and there were weeks when things felt more manageable. Sofia loves our child and has turned out to be a good parent. Ultimately, though, we were more like roommates than romantic partners and that wasn't enough for me. Our core issues never got resolved.

When I finally decided to file for divorce, all those issues about who, what, and when to tell resurfaced again. I needed support and wanted to tell my friends and family that we were divorcing, but Sofia wanted everything to be kept private. I finally decided I could tell whoever I wanted about *my* experience without going into what was going on with Sofia. That felt like freedom to me.

Thankfully, we have worked out a great co-parenting relationship and our child is doing well. I'm in a new relationship, and the communication between us is so much better. I feel like I learned a lot from my marriage about what I need from a partner. I just found out I am pregnant again. This time around, I'm going to shout it from the rooftops!

Can You Relate?

Put a check mark next to the sentences you relate to.

- ☐ I really needed a partner, but instead, I felt so alone.
- ☐ I felt like I was on an emotional rollercoaster all by myself.
- ☐ When I worried my body was failing me, the person I needed the most was totally absent.
- ☐ I kept hoping that once the baby arrived, things would be better.
- ☐ I never realized what an impact in-laws could have on a marriage.
- ☐ Having a baby was so important that I was going to go through with it no matter what.

Oona's Notes

- For LGBTQ+ couples, differences in each partner's comfort level with their sexuality can cause ongoing conflict.
- Fertility treatments (and many other medical procedures) can be financially, physically, and emotionally taxing, creating distance and conflict between couples.

- When there's misalignment in how much couples want to share with friends and family, both spouses can end up feeling they're not getting their needs met.

- Lack of family support can negatively impact a marriage, especially if the couple has children. Despite the gains that have been made, many LGBTQ+ couples do not have family support.

- Lesbians marry and divorce more frequently than gay men and at a roughly equivalent rate to heterosexual couples. Lesbians divorce for many of the same reasons heterosexual couples do. Additional factors include women moving in and marrying more quickly, lack of family support, and stress from stigma and discrimination.

Exercise: **Looking Back**

Family dynamics play a big role in any marriage and often create stress and conflict. Reflect on the roles of your family and your spouse's family in your marriage by considering the following:

How was your relationship with your in-laws during your marriage?

_____

_____

_____

_____

What do you wish was different about that relationship?

_____

_____

_____

How did your relationship with them impact your marriage?

_____

_____

_____

3

Following the Map

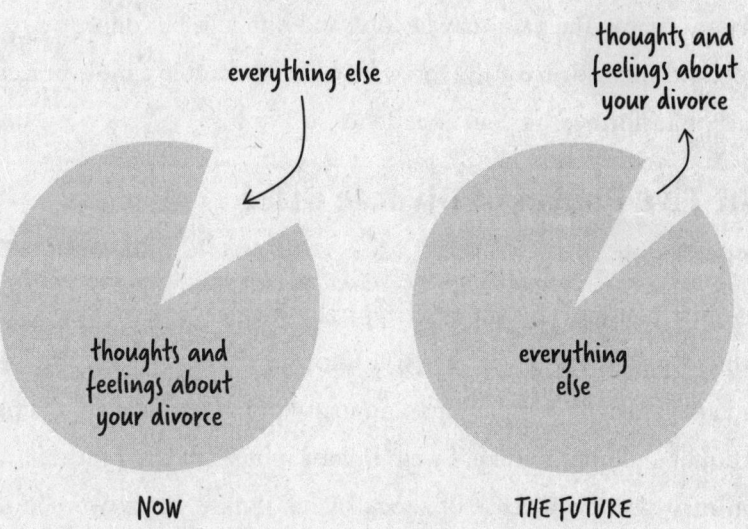

Divorce brings up intense feelings for everyone. Because each marriage and divorce is unique, it's impossible to predict exactly how and when you'll have these emotions. Yet there are common themes and emotional patterns in what women tend to experience that will help guide you. Use this chapter as a map for the emotional arc of your divorce.

Elisabeth Kübler-Ross developed a model of grief that is still widely used today to understand emotional responses to death. Her model includes five stages: denial, anger, bargaining, depression, and acceptance. Many divorce professionals use her model as a way to explain the phases of divorce grief. However, I have found that it doesn't fully capture the experiences of the women I see in my practice. In order to provide a more relevant option, I have developed a five phase model of divorce grief. My hope is that it will help you navigate this process, providing a general road map for the healing process. You may find that some phases overlap or you return to earlier stages before moving forward again. The path may be long and difficult, but once you have processed your divorce grief, you will eventually land in a more peaceful place, transformed by your experience.

The Five Phases of Divorce Grief
Heartbreak

The first phase of divorce grief typically involves intense anger and sadness, regardless of whether you initiated the divorce or not. Loss and grief are daily companions, and many women experience a period of doubt and questioning as well. If your spouse initiated the divorce, you may also feel a sense of shock or numbness. Many women describe feeling blindsided, as if the rug has been pulled out from under them, a tornado has landed in their living room, or their foundation has been shaken. In addition to emotional pain, you may experience physical symptoms, including changes in sleep, appetite, energy, and concentration. If you initiated the divorce, it is likely you have felt your heart breaking many times over the years, every time you were not seen, heard, or valued.

Rollercoaster

The middle of divorce grief is often the longest phase. Just like when you ride an actual rollercoaster, there are many ups and downs, a few calmer straightaways, times you will feel out of control, and a sense of relief when the ride ends. But unlike a literal rollercoaster, no one finishes their divorce and shouts, "I wanna do that again!" Instead, you will feel immense relief when your divorce is over, and vow never to do it again.

During this phase, you'll undoubtedly experience a whirlwind of emotions, so much so that you may wonder if you're going crazy. It's not unusual to feel sad, angry, fearful, frustrated, worried, regretful, hurt, rejected, ashamed, confused, *and* relieved, sometimes all in the same day. Emotions will come and go in both expected and unexpected ways. You may find you have two seemingly opposite feelings simultaneously. For example, you might be angry at your ex *and* miss them. Or feel lonely and sad *and* relieved to have space. In this phase especially, it is crucial to develop a good support system and a self-care plan that works for you. See Chapters 3 and 6 for more self-care strategies.

Mending

Your emotions become less intense and less frequent as you mend your broken heart. This phase represents a shift in focus away from your ex and toward yourself. You may still feel sad and angry, but you'll also experience greater relief as you move further from the conflict and tension in your marriage. Your relationship with your ex, your family, and friends may get renegotiated as you seek new connections and create new boundaries. This is also a period of reflection and taking responsibility for your part in your marriage and divorce. While you're mending, don't be surprised if you find yourself back in the Rollercoaster phase from time to time.

Letting Go

This important phase marks the time when you accept that your marriage is over and let go of your identity as a married person. In this phase, you begin to feel calmer as you move out of limbo and into your new life with more certainty. No longer so activated by your ex, you will experience greater peace. With more energy for non-divorce-related activities, you may feel ready to start dating again. Like in the Mending phase, many women renegotiate boundaries with friends, family, and work during this period. The story of your marriage will evolve to include deeper understanding and shared responsibility. You'll begin to forgive yourself, those close to you, and maybe even your ex.

Moving On

In this last phase, your marriage and divorce feel more firmly in the past. While they'll always be part of your history, they no longer dominate your daily life. You can expect a return to normal during this phase, but it won't be the normal of the past. This will be a new kind of normal in which your post-divorce identity will emerge as you embrace what you need and want in life. As you regain power and control, you'll have energy to develop new interests or return to past ones. You may feel ready for partnership or cherish your time alone. Many women go from feeling their divorce was the worst thing that could happen to thinking of it as a painful but necessary change that actually improved their lives. In this phase, you know you've survived and feel ready to thrive.

> *Once grief has occupied space in your life, it never entirely leaves. It may sit silently at times, but it is always there because it's connected to something significant that's had a lasting impact on your life.*
>
> **Eleanor Haley and Litsa Williams**

Exercise: **Goal Setting**

This is a version of the goal-setting exercise that I use with members of my divorce support group when I first meet with them.

First, identify which phase of divorce grief you are currently in: Heartbreak, Rollercoaster, Mending, Letting Go, or Moving On. Write down your current phase here: _____.

Next, reflect on where you are emotionally in regard to your marriage, separation, or divorce. Write down today's date and three feeling words that best describe your current emotional state. Here are some examples to get you started.

- I feel hopeless, angry, and unsteady today.
- I feel sad, lonely, and worried today.
- I feel rejected, ashamed, and confused today.

Date: _____

1. _____
2. _____
3. _____

Then, write down three ways you *want* to feel about your situation a year from now. These are your twelve-month goals.

Here are some examples to get you started:

- I want to feel hopeful, calm, and steady a year from now.
- I want to feel happy, connected, and relaxed a year from now.
- I want to feel lovable, confident, and clear a year from now.

Now write three for yourself.

1. _____
2. _____
3. _____

Congratulations on setting your goals! You get extra points if you share these with a friend or write them down where you can easily find them. You get extra points *and* a gold star if you look at your goals from time to time and track your progress over the next year.

How Long Does It Take to Get Divorced?

Most people never consider the steps of divorce or how long it takes until they have to. What I can tell you about the legal proceedings is it will probably take longer than you'd like. Please don't believe anyone who gives you an exact time frame. I have seen divorces be finalized in as quickly as four months (though that's rare) and some that last four years (also rare). Differences in timing mostly depend on how much the two parties agree or disagree about the division of assets and the parenting plan.

Your divorce should proceed more quickly if you don't have children (or your children are grown and out of the house) and your assets are limited or straightforward. Parenting plans and asset division can take time to negotiate. If you have an amicable relationship, an agreement on how to divide assets, and a legal team who values resolution, your divorce will likely proceed more quickly. If you aren't aligned on a parenting schedule, have major disagreements about assets, or have attorneys who belabor even the smallest points, it will likely take longer. If your spouse is very passive, antagonizing, controlling, or deceitful, your divorce may also drag on, as those traits are not conducive to cooperative, timely negotiations.

You'll find that there is a legal arc of divorce and an emotional arc of divorce. Many women in the Letting Go phase feel much better when their legal proceedings are complete. Others feel better before the legalities are finalized. Women who are locked in co-parenting conflicts or have other extenuating circumstances may struggle to reach the Letting Go phase, even after the legal process is over. It's hard to predict how long it takes to heal from a divorce, but you'll see signs along the way and you'll know once you've arrived.

Women in my support group who reach the Moving On phase say things like:

- "I got an email from my ex and I didn't feel dread and doom."
- "Last week I didn't think about my ex at all."
- "I felt attracted to someone in the fruit aisle of the grocery store."
- "I'm really looking forward to having this weekend all to myself."
- "I picked up a brush and painted the garage and it looks great."

When you notice yourself feeling independent, empowered, strong, attractive, capable, *even for a moment,* those are signs of progress. You will know you have reached the Moving On phase when you can say your divorce is part of your history but no longer a daily concern.

Will You Ever Get Over Your Divorce?

If you mean will your divorce disappear from your memory or cease to be part of your history? Probably not. But will you get through the hurdles of divorce and land safely on the other side of it? Almost certainly. Will you make meaning from it? Of course you will. Grow, learn, change, evolve? Yes, absolutely. The fact that you are reading this book shows you are already moving through the phases of grief. If you're like many of the women I work with, you may even find your divorced life is better than your married life. Your divorce will always be part of who you are and your history. What will diminish is the turmoil it has caused and the space it takes up in your brain.

When women first join my support groups, they're usually in the Heartbreak or Rollercoaster phase. They welcome the chance to connect with others and are grateful to have a place to talk about their divorce *every single week*. As time goes on, however, and they work through the phases of grief, many no longer want to focus their time, energy, and finances on talking about their divorce every week. Instead, as they approach the Moving On phase, they prefer to use the time they'd spent in the group to date, take a yoga class, go to graduate school, or just enjoy their free time. They leave the group transformed, empowered, and more independent than when they started—ready to move on. That is the goal. I have worked with hundreds of women who have reached this phase, and I know you can get there, too.

Mandy's Story

*"Not being able to trust the person
I married was terrible, but not being able
to trust myself was even worse."*

I met Jeff at work when we were both in our late twenties. He was married and had a baby at the time. When we met, he told me he was separated from his wife. He described her as controlling and critical and told me he couldn't wait to be divorced. I was hesitant to date a married man, but he reassured me they were practically divorced—just a matter of signing a few papers—and I went along with it.

If only I had known then what I know now.

Jeff was extremely outgoing and always the life of the party. He had expensive taste, wore beautifully tailored suits, and drove a fancy car. At the beginning, I was completely smitten. He brought me flowers and took me to expensive restaurants. I'll never forget how a month after we started dating, he gave me diamond earrings. My friends were jealous of our relationship as their boyfriends weren't as generous as Jeff. At the time, he made me feel so special. He constantly said he adored me and showed me off to his friends.

I didn't think too much about the fact that we never went to his place. My apartment was closer to our office, so it was convenient for him to stay with me. I asked a few times to see his place, but then something would come up and he'd cancel. After four months, I still hadn't seen where he lived and started to get a nagging feeling. One night when he was away on a work trip, I decided to drive by, just to see what his house looked like. That's when I saw his wife and son through the living room window. I had to drive by his house three more times just to convince myself of what I was seeing.

When I discovered that first lie, I felt like I was having an out-of-body experience.

I should have left him that night. It was clear he was still living with his wife—they were far from divorced or even separated. But Jeff was persistent. He sent dozens of flowers with long apology letters. He begged, pleaded, and gave me a big story about being so ashamed he was living with his wife that he couldn't bear to tell me. He promised they were over. I tried to resist, but he was so focused on winning me back that eventually I caved. I insisted he couldn't live with his wife if we were going to continue to date, and he did finally move out.

It took Jeff a whole year after that to get divorced. The day after he went to court, he proposed to me at our favorite restaurant. He turned it into a big event, secretly inviting all our friends and family and even hiring a videographer to capture the moment. The ring was gorgeous and I said yes. He was definitely the most charming man I'd ever met and I got swept up in the romance of it all.

We bought a big house in the suburbs and settled down. Jeff said I could quit my job and he would finance our life, but I liked working so I stayed at our company. He thought we divided our household tasks equally. In reality, he had no idea what it took to keep a household running. He took care of our finances and our cars, but I basically did all the cleaning, shopping, house chores, and social planning. I learned early on that Jeff didn't like to do any tasks that he considered "menial." He golfed most weekends and I ended up caring for his son when he stayed with us.

In addition to being a part-time stepmother, I wanted kids of my own, and I got pregnant pretty easily. Before that, Jeff and I had shared a good sex life. He definitely had a higher sex drive, but I was into it, too. Then things changed.

During my pregnancy, I didn't want to have sex.

Jeff got really upset and threw these mini tantrums. After our daughter was born, I was too tired to have sex and my drive was low. When our daughter was two months old, I caught him cheating on me with our neighbor. I was devastated and enraged. I felt betrayed by both of them and so angry that their affair was taking my attention away from our baby.

He blamed me for his affair, saying he had sexual needs I wasn't meeting. I was too exhausted to even consider leaving him, and he promised he would never betray me again. I forgave him eventually, but it changed the way I felt about being intimate with him. Plus, working and doing 95 percent of the childcare didn't leave me feeling very sexy.

Even though we survived that betrayal, I never fully regained my trust.

Jeff got fired from a number of jobs when our daughter was young. He wasn't good at following rules and couldn't get along with his bosses. He always said, "Rules are made for the little people." He resented being told what to do and complained that he should be paid more. Despite some fairly long periods of unemployment, Jeff continued to be a big spender.

He finally got a job where he was the boss, managing a sales team. One woman on the team was twenty years younger, and Jeff started golfing with her on the weekends. I was anxious about their connection, but he insisted they were "just friends." He spent more and more time with her, and every once in a while, I would catch him in a lie. Over time, he became more distant, cold, and critical. I noticed he was spending more time at the gym, working out every day. I knew he was vain, but he became completely obsessed with his looks.

I was suspicious, but I hated feeling like a spy, so I tried to just focus on the good parts of our marriage.

Near the end of our marriage, Jeff told me he was going on a work trip to Ohio. When he was supposed to be on that trip, my friend ran into him on the beach in Miami with his younger co-worker. She called to tell me, and I had that same sensation I'd had years before when I drove by his house—that I was having an out-of-body experience. This one hit especially hard because he got caught red-handed and still denied it. For me, the lying was worse than him having sex with someone else. He made up a story that they went to Miami for work and he didn't tell me because he knew I'd be mad. I was mad all right.

I started seeing a therapist because I felt like my head was on backward. I didn't know who or what to believe. What else was he lying about? Who could I trust? I doubted myself, and my self-esteem took a major hit.

Not being able to trust the person I married was terrible, but not being able to trust myself was even worse.

After only a few sessions, my therapist asked if anyone had ever diagnosed my husband with narcissism and if I'd heard of love bombing. I went home that night and read everything I could find on cycles of narcissistic abuse. Everything started to make sense. It was like he was operating from a narcissism textbook. On the one hand, it was devastating to learn this about him, but on the other, it made me feel less crazy and alone. The books I read said it was unlikely he would change, but it was still hard to give up on the life we had built together.

In the end, Jeff was the one who decided to leave me. His decision seemed abrupt even though he had been treating me terribly for years. He filed for divorce while I was in the hospital recovering from a minor surgery. It was a cruel way to do it, but that was Jeff. Our divorce was brutal. It's like the divorce took his worst personal qualities of not following rules and not caring about my needs and magnified them by a hundred. Even though he filed for divorce, he wouldn't complete the financial paperwork. He yelled at his lawyers and made up crazy stories about my mental health to try to get his way. He even stormed out of the courtroom at one point. To top it off, he tried to hide his retirement account overseas. It was stunning to see what lengths he went to just to portray himself as the victim.

I'm still recovering from my marriage and my divorce, but I've made a lot of progress. My therapist has been really helpful, and I joined a support group of women who are divorcing narcissists. Those women are my lifeline. I have learned so much from them. I'll never forget getting served divorce papers in my hospital room and thinking it was the worst day of my life. As it turns out, it was actually one of the best things that could have happened. Now that I know Jeff is never going to change, I can stop trying to make our marriage better. I am finally free of all the emotional abuse I lived with for so long. I'm not ready to date yet, but I know exactly what to look out for when I do. Until then, I'm enjoying being on my own.

Can You Relate?

Put a check mark next to the sentences you relate to.

- ☐ If only I had known then what I know now.

- ☐ When I discovered that first lie, I felt like I was having an out-of-body experience.

- ☐ During my pregnancy, I didn't want to have sex.

- ☐ Even though we survived that betrayal, I never fully regained my trust.

- ☐ I was suspicious, but I hated feeling like a spy, so I tried to just focus on the good parts of our marriage.

- ☐ Not being able to trust the person I married was terrible, but not being able to trust myself was even worse.

Oona's Notes

- Love bombing is often the first stage of a narcissistic abuse cycle. It involves intense flattery, expensive gifts, jealousy, and pressure for commitment.

- Discovering a partner has been deceitful can be traumatic. Some people experience depersonalization symptoms, feeling as if they're disconnected from their body and watching it from the outside.

- One hallmark of people with narcissistic traits is that they can be incredibly charming and socially adept.

- Another hallmark of people with narcissistic traits is their sense of entitlement and belief that they are too important to complete menial tasks.

- Narcissists have difficulty taking responsibility for their own actions and often blame others for their behavior.

- People with narcissistic traits often have difficulty with authority and trouble following rules.

- A sudden increase in working out and an intense focus on looks can be a sign of infidelity.

- "Gaslighting" refers to psychological manipulation of a person over time, leading them to doubt their own perception of reality. It can cause confusion, insecurity, and dependence.

- While every divorce is challenging, divorcing a narcissist can be particularly difficult. Many narcissists lack empathy, are entitled and exploitative, and feel the rules do not apply to them.

Narcissistic Personality Disorder

Narcissistic Personality Disorder, or NPD, is a diagnosable mental health condition with the following behavior patterns:

- A lack of empathy for others
- A need for excessive admiration from others
- A grandiose sense of self-importance
- A sense of entitlement
- A preoccupation with themselves
- Exploitative behavior that takes advantage of others
- A sense of arrogance or superiority
- Fantasies of success, power, beauty, brilliance
- Envy of others

People who meet the criteria for Narcissistic Personality Disorder display at least five of the nine behaviors above. Some people demonstrate narcissistic behaviors, but do not meet the criteria for a full diagnosis. If your spouse has been diagnosed with Narcissistic Personality Disorder or you simply recognize some of the behaviors listed above, it may be useful to do further research on narcissism. (See Resources for a list of books.) Many narcissists behave as if they are operating from a textbook, with clear and predictable behavior patterns. Identifying and recognizing those patterns and learning specific communication strategies to deal with them can be immensely helpful. We'll be diving into communication strategies more fully in Chapter 9.

The Narcissistic Abuse Cycle

The narcissistic abuse cycle is an informal model that resonates with many survivors of abuse. It refers to a harmful pattern of behaviors in which someone attempts to manipulate and exploit another person. This cycle often includes four stages:

- **Idealization:** This stage involves appreciation, adoration, and love bombing, all designed to charm you.

- **Devaluation:** This stage may include passive-aggressive behavior, criticism, stonewalling, lack of empathy, ridicule, humiliation, and defensiveness. The narcissist might use gaslighting to accuse you of things you didn't do, causing you to question your own perceptions.

- **Discard:** After the narcissist has subjected you to a repeating cycle of idealization and devaluation, they may decide they no longer need you. During this stage, some narcissists may be especially abrupt, cold, dismissive, and unempathetic. Others never fully discard their partners.

- **Reengagement:** After discarding you, some narcissists may try to reengage with you in order to start the cycle all over again. This stage is often referred to as the "Hoover stage," as the narcissist attempts to suck you back in, just like a vacuum cleaner.

Love Bombing

Love bombing often occurs at the beginning of a relationship with a narcissist. The narcissist's goal is control, not love, and they attempt to manipulate their partner using the following tactics:

- Intense, early declarations of love
- Overwhelming attention and compliments
- Frequent communication via texts, calls, etc.
- Disregarding boundaries (unwillingness to accept "no")
- Need for constant validation
- Expensive or over-the-top gifts
- Jealousy or annoyance if you're not available
- Inability to take responsibility for their hurtful words or actions in current or past relationships

Exercise: Love Bombing True-or-False Quiz

See how much you know about love bombing by taking this true-false quiz.

1. The only people who fall victim to love bombing are either weak or oblivious. **T/F**

2. It's a red flag for someone to tell you they love you or you are their soulmate on your first or second date. **T/F**

3. Narcissists typically lack social skills. **T/F**

4. People who use love bombing tactics often disregard personal boundaries. **T/F**

5. People who are diagnosed with Narcissistic Personality Disorder are good candidates for talk therapy and can be treated with medication for their diagnosis. **T/F**

1. **False.** Many strong, smart, successful people have fallen victim to love bombing tactics, as these behaviors often feel loving and romantic at first. 2. **True.** It is a red flag if someone tells you they love you or you are their soulmate before they really know you. True love happens as two people get to know each other over time. Declaring love before knowing someone may be an early sign of love bombing. 3. **False.** Most narcissists have excellent social skills and are considered to be charming and charismatic. They are usually most charming in public settings and often act vastly different in private. 4. **True.** Love bombers disregard personal boundaries as they seek control. They may show up uninvited, call or text incessantly, seek personal information too quickly, and/or disregard boundaries. 5. **False.** There is no medication specifically designed to treat Narcissistic Personality Disorder. Many narcissists are reluctant to engage in talk therapy as they have difficulty showing vulnerability and blame others for their problems.

4

Sharing Your Location

Divorce is a heavy burden to carry by yourself. Once you know you're going to separate or divorce, you'll want to tell the important people in your life about this transition. This can be overwhelming and emotional, so it's important to pace yourself. Confiding in others is an important step in your journey and helps pave the way for support.

Who, What, and When to Tell People About Your Divorce

Rest assured, there is no rush or correct timeline for sharing the news. You don't have to tell everyone at once, *nor should you give everyone the same amount of information.* But having a plan will help you feel less overwhelmed. I encourage you to be very thoughtful about what details you decide to share.

> **You can always tell people more of the story later, but you can never untell the details of your divorce.**

Shouting from the rooftops might sound appealing, especially if you're feeling angry or betrayed, but I'd urge you to wait until your logical brain has caught up with your emotions. You don't want to do anything that will damage your relationships, your legal case, or your own sense of self. Several women in my groups have reported feeling enraged when they learned about their spouse's infidelity. Their heightened emotions made them unable to slow down enough to think about who and what to tell. Later on, they ended up feeling exposed and regretted not taking the time to cool off and make thoughtful decisions.

Remember, *you can always decide to share more details later, but once they are out, you cannot erase the tape.* Think about what we tell our kids about posting on social media—the internet lives forever!

Telling Your Children

Every parent dreads this conversation. It is one of the most difficult in any divorce, as it means sharing heartbreaking news with your children. We are all programmed to nurture and protect our kids, so this step may feel like it goes against our parental instincts. And yet being a parent also means being honest and responsible. That includes letting your children know about changes to your family's life. What's more, you are your children's most important role model. In sharing this news, you have an opportunity to demonstrate both vulnerability and resilience. It's important to communicate a balance of "this is a sad time" *and* "we are going to get through this."

You may need to talk to a few people for support before telling your children about your divorce, but if you do, be sure those people are *extremely trustworthy*. Your children deserve to hear about your divorce from you personally, not from a friend who heard it from his mom.

Ideally, you'll tell all your children in person at once, but that may not be possible if one or more of them is at college, studying abroad, or away at camp, for example. Try to avoid asking your children to keep your news a secret, especially from their siblings. That puts too much pressure on them in an already stressful situation.

The best-case scenario is you and your spouse sitting down together to develop a script for this conversation. Not a script that you read, but an agreed-upon set of statements. However, if your spouse is unwilling, absent, or can't be relied on, you'll have to tell the children yourself. While this is not ideal, it is sometimes the reality. Hearing the news from one thoughtful, rational parent is better than hearing it from two people who can't agree on what to say, or who end up saying hurtful things to each other or their children.

Timing the Conversation

The timing of this conversation will be influenced by several factors. In general, it's better to tell older kids sooner rather than later because they're more likely to pick up on tension in the house and overhear your conversations. It's also best if you have information about any upcoming changes in housing before you sit down with them to talk.

Older kids who have witnessed a lot of fighting, a toxic environment, or emotional abuse may feel relieved you are finally ending an unhealthy cycle. I'd recommend waiting to tell much younger children until a housing change is imminent. Younger children can't track time the way adults do, so sharing changes to the family well in advance won't serve them. If one of you is moving out, tell younger kids no more than a few weeks beforehand.

It's important that you don't use your children as confidants, as tempting and convenient as that might be. Resist the urge to talk with them about the problems in your marriage or how you feel about your spouse. Telling kids you are thinking about a divorce *next year* or that you *might* divorce can create anxiety for them. Wait until you have information that is relevant to *their lives*.

When timing the conversation, try to avoid other big transitions in their lives, like mourning a death, graduating from high school or college, starting the school year, or leaving for summer camp. Of course, there is no perfect time to share this difficult news, and you may have little control over the timing. However, do whatever is in your power to ease kids into the transition.

If your child asks if you're going to get divorced when your spouse is not present, acknowledge their question and tell them you're planning a family meeting to talk more. Make sure that family conversation happens as soon as possible (that night or the next day) so your child does not carry the weight of uncertainty for too long. If you're not completely ready or there are more details to work out, you might say, "It's been hard lately, but we are working together to figure out the best path forward. We will keep you posted about any changes to our family as we always do."

What to Say

Many parents worry about what to say, how to say it, and what impact it will have on their children. You may feel pressure to "get it right" or "say it all" during this first conversation. While it *is* important to be thoughtful about how you share the news, keep in mind that you will be talking to your children *many times over many years* about the divorce. For this initial conversation, less is more.

Because this is your children's first time hearing the news, and because you'll likely be in an emotional place, it's best to keep the conversation brief. You can always add more details later. Once you've said your part, let them react and ask questions. Be prepared with answers to their questions. Let them leave the room if they need to. You can check on them after a few minutes to remind them you're still available to hear their thoughts and feelings.

The Five Elements of a Divorce Conversation with Children

- **Start with the fact that you have decided to divorce.** This can be just one sentence. It is best to say, "We have decided to divorce," even if only one of you initiated the decision. If you think there is a chance of reconciliation after a trial separation, use the word "separate" instead of "divorce."

- **Be thoughtful about how you explain the reasons for the divorce.** Children do not need to know the intimate details about why you are getting divorced, and in fact, knowing those details could be hard on them. But they *do* need a reason. "We haven't been getting along" or "We are no longer making each other happy" are good options to help simplify a complicated situation. Make sure to reassure them that your divorce is not their fault.

- **Let them know you've tried to make things better.** This is important, as you want your children to know that you value your family and tried to work on your marriage. It also sends the message that when your children face hard things in their lives, they should also do their best to make them better.

- **Offer reassurance about what will and will not change in their lives.** Make sure to emphasize one thing that will not change is your love for them. If you know other things that will or will not change (their home, school, schedule), mention those as well. Don't make promises unless you know you can keep them.

- **Finish up by normalizing their feelings and inviting them to talk to you at any time.** This is crucial. Just as your feelings about the divorce will shift over time, so will theirs. Your children need to know they can come to you at any time to talk about their feelings and ask questions.

Here are two examples that incorporate these five elements:

Grace and Tony—Telling Their Kids

Grace and Tony were married for fifteen years when they decided to divorce. They had an eight-year-old daughter and a fourteen-year-old son. Despite Tony's ongoing affair, Grace was determined not to blame him when she talked to her children. She was angry with Tony but wanted to preserve the kids' relationship with their father. They waited until Tony found an apartment to talk with their kids.

One Saturday morning, they sat the kids down in the living room. Grace did most of the talking: "We want to let you know that we've decided to get a divorce. We have been unhappy for a while and have tried to make our relationship better, but it hasn't worked. We are still your parents, and we love you very much—that will never change. What will change is that Dad is going to move into an apartment next month. You will still live here with me for now, and you will get to see your dad every week. We know this may be upsetting and surprising, and we want you to know that it is normal to have all kinds of feelings. We are here for you if you want to talk about any of them."

When Grace and Tony finished, their daughter started crying and pleaded with them not to get divorced. Though Grace was heartbroken, she knew it was important to be strong for her daughter. She responded, "I can see how sad you are, honey. Do you want to come sit in my lap?" Their son showed no emotion and responded, "Can we get a gaming system at Dad's apartment?" Tony paused, then replied, "We have a lot of changes in our family right now. We're going to do our best to take care of everyone, but we'll have to see."

You can see here that Grace and Tony used the Five Elements to talk to their children. They started with the facts, were thoughtful about how much information they shared, made it clear they'd tried to work on the marriage, provided reassurance, and normalized their kids' feelings.

Their children had different reactions, but both were normal and appropriate. Their daughter was more direct about her feelings, which was her usual style. Their son, in keeping with his personality, was more guarded. His initial reaction was concern about his gaming system. While some parents may hear that as a selfish statement, I hear his concern as his way of expressing loss: "Will I lose access to an activity I love? Will I lose my dad? What else will I lose?" Grace and Tony did a great job sharing the news.

Sarah and Denise—Telling Their Daughter

Sarah and Denise couldn't afford a second apartment after deciding to separate, but they were miserable spending so much time together. They decided to continue living together until they could afford a second place. While they weren't pursuing divorce yet, they felt it was necessary to communicate this change in their family system to their daughter.

After dinner one night, they began: "We know you have heard your mom and me arguing a lot lately. We want you to know we've gotten help for our arguments, but we've decided we can't be happy living in the same house anymore. We are still figuring out how to live separately, but for now, Mom is going to move into the guest room and Mama will stay in our bedroom. We're going to be spending more time with you one-on-one

> instead of the three of us together. We'll let you know when we decide to make any more changes. We love you very much and want to be sure you know this isn't your fault. We understand how sad this is and that you may have a lot of other feelings as well. You can come talk about this with us at any time."

Sarah and Denise decided to be open and honest about their relationship status, despite not knowing when their housing would change. They effectively used the Five Elements of a divorce conversation. They started with the facts, were vague about the reason, shared their efforts to get along better, provided reassurance, and normalized their daughter's feelings.

Once you've shared the news with your children using the Five Elements, *stop talking*. Provide space for their reactions and questions. Depending on your children's ages and personalities, they may respond with anger, sadness, anxiety, or relief. They may burst into tears or blame one of you or each other. They may storm out of the room or the house. Or they may act as if nothing has happened and ask what's for dinner. All of these reactions are normal. Reflect back to them how they feel or what you imagine they might be feeling.

Here are some examples:

- "I can see how sad you are. It's okay to cry, this is a sad day."

- "I hear how mad you are. I know this isn't what you wanted."

- "I can see how shocking this news is to you. It'll take some time to sink in."

Resist the urge to make the divorce sound rosy or like it's a good idea. This is not the time to say, "Look on the bright side, you'll get to have two Christmases!" For now, just try to empathize with what your children are feeling. Don't be dismissive of their feelings and don't minimize the news. As hard as it is, try to create a container for your children's emotions, holding them tenderly. That way, your children will feel seen and heard by you, two fundamental building blocks in the healing process.

Finally, don't make promises unless you are 100 percent sure you can keep them. For example, many parents make the mistake of telling their kids they'll always live in their childhood home, or they'll always have Christmas together as a family. I know you feel guilty and want to soften the blow, but it's very hard to predict the future when you're starting your divorce. It's much better to talk about what you know to be true *at this moment*. Other than reassuring them your love for them will never change, leave the future out of it for now.

Exercise: Write Your Script

Write a couple of drafts of what you'll tell your children about your separation or divorce. Be sure to incorporate the Five Elements:

- Start with the fact that you have decided to separate or divorce.

- Be vague with the details about *why* you're separating or getting a divorce.

- Let them know that you've tried to make things better.

- Provide a lot of reassurance about what will and will not change in your children's lives, including your love for them.

- Finish up by normalizing your children's feelings and inviting them to talk to you at any time.

_____
_____
_____
_____
_____
_____
_____

Once you have your script written, practice saying it aloud a few times until you can get through it without crying too much or blaming your spouse. We can't always control our emotions, but do try to strike a balance. Showing no emotion at all does not reflect the reality of what you are saying. Expressing too many emotions may cause your children to feel unsafe, or that there isn't enough room for their feelings. I know that's easier said than done, but I also know you can do this. Go easy on yourself—the goal here is not perfection. This is a particularly hard moment in your divorce journey. And remember, this is the first of many conversations you'll be having with your children about the divorce.

Telling Your Friends, Family, and Colleagues

Visualize a ring of people, with you in the middle and three (or more) circles around you. Each circle represents a different category of people in your life. You will have different versions of your story for the people in each of those categories.

The innermost circle includes the people you are closest to—perhaps a few friends and family members who know you well. Let's call this circle **Close Allies**.

The next circle includes people who are important to you, but with whom you don't share the *most* personal details of your life. These may be colleagues or more distant family members, certain friends, maybe parents of your kids' friends. We will call this circle **Friendly Comrades**.

And then there is the outer circle—more distant colleagues, your favorite barista, your plumber, your kid's soccer coach, your nosy neighbor. These people might know that you're married, but they don't know much about your life. Let's call this circle **Neutral Nellies**.

Talking to your Close Allies about your divorce will play a crucial role in giving you the support you need. Your Close Allies are people who know you well and whom you trust with the most personal details of your life. You can be open and vulnerable with them. Plan to share as many details with them as feels comfortable. You may start out with only a couple of people, but as time goes on, you might find it's beneficial to include a wider group of friends in this inner circle.

While you may be having ongoing conversations with those closest to you, it can be helpful to plan ahead what you'll share with your middle circle, the Friendly Comrades. They may include your colleagues, and friends and family members who are not closest to you.

They know you, and may even know your spouse, but don't know the intimate details of your life.

It might make sense for you to tell Friendly Comrades yourself, or you may find that too draining. If the task feels too overwhelming, you can appoint a messenger to deliver the news instead.

> ### *Sharon—Telling Co-workers About Her Divorce*
>
> Sharon started a new job just before her divorce was finalized. Her friend Tracey worked at the same company. Sharon was excited to meet all her new colleagues, but she dreaded the inevitable question about her marital status. She asked Tracey to mention to her team that she was getting divorced, and while it was not necessarily a painful topic anymore, she would rather not discuss it at work. Tracey was happy to do this for Sharon, and their co-workers were understanding and respectful. Sharon was able to settle into her new job without worrying about being thrown off by distracting personal questions. Over time, she felt more comfortable referring to the divorce as an event in her past that didn't hold as much emotional charge anymore.

If you opt to tell people yourself, you may want to set aside a time for a planned conversation. Think carefully about which details you feel comfortable sharing and which you want to keep private. Of course, you won't be able to plan every conversation you have about your divorce. Many well-meaning Friendly Comrades and Neutral Nellies will unknowingly and innocently stumble into a conversation that touches on your marriage. It helps to be prepared for this. You can choose to answer vaguely and move on or answer succinctly and pivot the conversation back to them.

The Vague Answer

Vague answers can be used with Friendly Comrades or Neutral Nellies, depending on your relationship with them. Let's pretend for a moment that your spouse is named Jesse. Consider the mom at the hockey game who asks where Jesse is tonight, the church friend who innocently asks why they haven't seen Jesse around lately, a colleague at the company holiday party who asks how Jesse is doing, or an aunt who asks if you're going on a family vacation this year. In each encounter, you may or may not feel ready to disclose details about your personal life, and you shouldn't feel obligated to lie. It's fine to be vague if you don't want to get into it. Your replies might sound like this:

- "Jesse couldn't come to the game."
- "Jesse has been busy."
- "Jesse is doing fine."
- "Our vacation is up in the air right now."

Notice that in each of the examples above you are telling the truth but remaining vague about the details. People often use these kinds of responses in the beginning of a divorce or when emotions feel overwhelming.

The Succinct Answer and Pivot

Another good strategy for talking to your Friendly Comrades and Neutral Nellies is to plan out a response to the inevitable questions that will arise. Providing a brief statement you have crafted in advance, followed by a question that changes the subject, will help the conversation feel less awkward. Here are a couple of examples:

- "Jesse and I are separated, but the kids and I are doing just fine. I can't get into the details right now, but thanks for asking. How have you been?"

- "Jesse and I are going through a divorce. It's been tough, but I have tons of support. Thanks for asking. I'm looking forward to that committee meeting next week. Did you have any ideas for the agenda?"

- "Jesse and I have decided to separate, so we aren't planning any family trips right now. We're all doing okay, though. How about you? Are you planning any trips?"

Answering succinctly and then pivoting your attention to the person who is asking politely signals you don't want to get into details.

Janine—Coping with a Nosy Boss

Janine and Paul started divorce proceedings after Janine discovered Paul was having an affair with a co-worker. Janine decided to tell three of her closest friends all the details, but she didn't want to share everything with her other friends and colleagues.

One day, her boss asked about the "For Sale" sign in front of her house: "I see your house is for sale. I didn't realize you were moving." Janine responded, "Actually, we are getting a divorce, so I am moving across town." Her boss replied, "Oh, Janine, I am so sorry. I had no idea. What happened? You two always seemed to be such a great couple." Janine didn't want to go into the details, but she knew she needed to give some kind of answer to her boss. Luckily, she had prepared for this moment. "I know—surprising, right? But I am doing just fine, and I'm glad to be here focused on my work. I know we have that deadline coming up on Friday, right?" Janine's boss kept questioning her, "I'm just so surprised. How are your kids? Was this sudden?" Janine was prepared for the onslaught of questions and just kept pivoting the conversation back. "The kids are doing fine, and actually I am, too. That deadline on Friday needs to be completed by noon, right?" Janine's boss finally gave up and talked about the upcoming deadline. Janine felt relieved to have gotten through the conversation, keeping her emotions in check and her boss out of her personal life.

Janine used several good strategies to stay in control of telling her story. First, she reached out to her Close Allies so she'd have a comfortable place to talk about all the details. Next, she prepared for the inevitable innocent questions from Friendly Comrades and Neutral Nellies. Finally, she gave short answers and pivots when her boss approached her.

Exercise: **Four Rings**

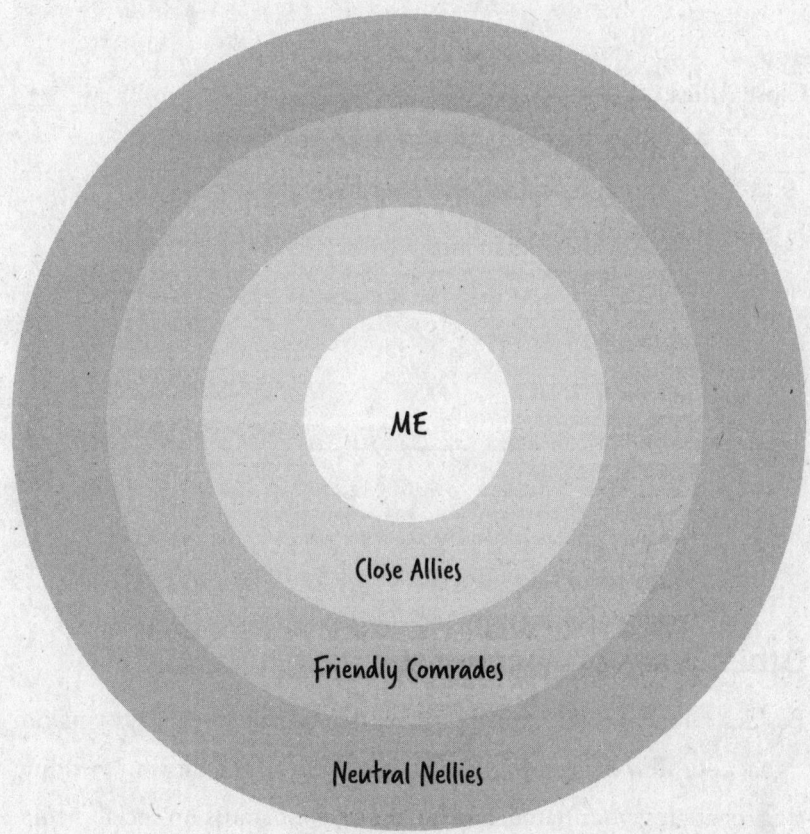

- First, list your Close Allies in the innermost ring. Write down what details you might share with your inner ring in the space below.

- Next, list your Friendly Comrades in the middle ring. Make a few notes about what you want to tell them. Think about who you want to have a planned conversation with.

- Finally, focus on your outer ring, your Neutral Nellies. Make a list of those people. Write down what you might say if the subject of your divorce comes up unexpectedly.

Close Allies: _____

_____

Friendly Comrades: _____

_____

Neutral Nellies: _____

_____

※ ※ ※

Other Ways of Sharing the News

Besides telling people directly, there are several other ways you can signal your new marital status. These include taking off your wedding ring, changing your name, and changing your status on social media.

Taking Off Your Ring

If you wear a wedding ring, taking it off can be a powerful and significant moment. Your wedding ring is a traditional symbol to the world that you are married—or not—and some people will notice the change. Some women take their wedding ring off when they know their marriage is emotionally over, and others wait until the legalities are finalized. The timing is up to you.

Some women buy themselves a divorce ring, something new that they always wanted or one they design themselves. If you decide to do this, feel free to wear your new ring on whatever finger feels best to you. You may decide to save your wedding ring for your child, repurpose it, or sell it to finance a trip. There is no right or wrong when it comes to what to do with your ring.

Changing Your Name

If you changed your name when you married, you'll have to decide whether to keep your married name, go back to your maiden name, or come up with a whole new last name. Some mothers want to keep their married name because it's shared with their children. For others, changing their name feels like a positive identity shift. This decision is highly personal, and you should do what feels right for you.

If you do decide to change your married name, know that there may be people in your life who assume you've gotten married rather than divorced. Depending on where you are emotionally, this can be jarring, upsetting, or just an annoyance. Add this faux pas to the list of things you won't do to other people now that you've been through a divorce.

Changing Your Status on Social Media

Just like taking off your wedding ring, there is no right or wrong time to change your status on social media; it's up to you to do it when the time feels right. It's usually a good idea to block or unfollow your ex as you move on from your marriage, as it will help with letting go. If you are connected to your ex's friends and family, you'll need to make decisions about whether to unfollow them as well. You may decide that keeping a connection with people associated with your ex is important to you or that you want privacy as you move into a new life. There is no one-size-fits-all formula here. Do whatever feels best for you.

New Terms for Your Ex

You may be wondering what to call your spouse now that you're getting divorced. Husband, wife, spouse, and ex all seem . . . not quite right. Here are some terms you can try:

- Their name
- My soon-to-be ex
- My former husband/wife/spouse
- My exiting husband/wife/spouse
- My child's father/mother/parent
- My co-parent
- My future ex
- My stbx (soon-to-be ex), commonly used in social media
- My was-band

Looking Ahead

So far, you've conquered the first leg of your divorce. You know about the three ways a divorce begins. You've thought about how to prepare yourself legally and financially and made to-do lists, including a self-care plan. You are thinking about the needs of your children. You are familiar with the Five Phases of Divorce Grief and know what to expect. You have shared the news with your family, friends, and colleagues and figured out who will be on your support team. You've already accomplished a lot! Take a few deep breaths and let that sink in. Good for you for making it this far.

I wish I could tell you the next stage of your divorce will be easy, but for most women, that is not the case. In Part Two, Climb the Mountain, we will walk together through some of the most challenging hills and valleys on your journey. You will have ups and downs, sometimes in the same week or the same hour, as you make your way through the Rollercoaster phase of divorce grief. There will be moments when your emotions feel all over the place, and at times, you may get overwhelmed. The good news is we'll discuss not only the variety of feelings you may experience in Chapter 5, but also concrete ways to care for yourself in Chapter 6.

You will meet Jada, who divorced Jimmy when she could no longer tolerate his alcoholism. Jada lived in divorce limbo for a long time, uncertain about her future.

Chapters 7 and 8 are devoted to helping your children through the transition of divorce. Feel free to skip those chapters if you don't have kids or read those chapters now if you need more information on supporting your kids right away. Go grab your water bottle and let's climb that mountain.

Part Two

Climb the Mountain

5

Staying on the Trail

There's a wonderful children's book by Michael Rosen and Helen Oxenbury called *We're Going on a Bear Hunt*. The book features a family that is going on a bear hunt but keeps running into obstacles that slow them down—grass, a river, mud, a forest, and finally a cave. The repeating refrain of the book is "We can't go over it. We can't go under it. Oh no! We've got to go through it." Despite their initial hesitations, they get through each hurdle until they find the bear.

This refrain reflects a cornerstone of mental health, one that's especially important when confronting a painful situation: You've got to go through it. As excruciating as it can be to experience *all the feelings* that come up during divorce, this is an essential step in the healing process.

Feeling All the Feels

Of course, you won't always have the capacity to confront your intense emotions. There will be times you are working, parenting, or socializing when you'll want to put them aside temporarily, and moments when distraction is useful and even healthy. But in general, it's perfectly normal and appropriate to experience a wide range of emotions during a divorce, including sadness, anger, fear, confusion, loneliness, regret, doubt, guilt, and shame.

Feelings are a fundamental part of being human and can provide valuable insight into your experience. Remember, your feelings aren't right or wrong; they just are. Just as you wouldn't let someone else tell you that you're not hot or hungry, don't let anyone tell you that you aren't sad or angry. Identifying and expressing how you feel will allow you to integrate your emotions and heal.

In the next few pages, we'll explore some of the most common divorce-related emotions. You'll probably experience them most intensely during the Heartbreak, Rollercoaster, and Mending phases; however, you may encounter them in the later phases of divorce grief as well.

Shock

"This can't be happening. I thought we were happy."

Women often experience profound disbelief and shock in the initial stages of divorce. If the end of your marriage wasn't your choice or came with little warning, it may be difficult to believe it's really happening. Shock is often accompanied by numbness or avoiding feeling anything at all.

You may be desperate to save your marriage or be confused, disoriented, and uncertain. Often women find that the change is so big and unexpected that it seems impossible to accept. You may find yourself shutting down, turning inward, and suppressing your feelings to protect yourself from the whirlwind that awaits.

Numbing and avoidance might seem preferable to overwhelming pain, but it's not healthy to avoid your feelings forever. Confronting your reality is a courageous and necessary process. Healing cannot happen without first acknowledging your pain and dealing with your emotions.

> While he was on a work trip, Leslie's husband sent her a text ending their thirty-year marriage. Leslie was stunned—she thought they were happy. She spent the next two months in a state of shock and denial. She didn't feel angry or sad or much of anything at first because she couldn't process the fact that her marriage was actually ending. Leslie experienced a sense of numbness, as if she were walking through thick fog. Every morning when she woke up, she was struck—again—with the reality that her marriage was over, as if she were experiencing it for the first time.

Affirmation
I will breathe through the shock of my situation.
I am breathing in, I am breathing out.

Guilt

"I'm constantly worried about how this divorce will impact my kids."

No matter how your divorce began, you may be feeling a great deal of guilt. Women especially struggle with self-blame as there's such a strong societal push for women to keep families intact. If your spouse wants to stay married, they're likely experiencing a lot of intense emotions, which may increase your feelings of guilt. If you have children, you may feel responsible for the inevitable changes they'll face. While guilt can be painful, it can also be a helpful emotion in guiding your future choices. For example, if you're feeling guilty about the impact of your divorce on your kids, make sure you do all you can to support them through the process. I encourage you to wrestle with your own sense of guilt to ensure you aren't being too harsh with yourself. Take a moment to think about how you would talk to your best friend if she were in your shoes.

> Jaclyn told her husband, Syd, she wanted a divorce after fifteen years of marriage. Despite being sure their marriage was over, she felt immense guilt when her husband reacted by begging and pleading with her to change her mind. She worried that her kids would be damaged by the divorce or would hate her for leaving their father. Syd tried everything to get her to stay, including telling her their children's lives would be ruined. Jaclyn held steady by making daily phone calls to her best friend, who reminded her why she was leaving. She

> also made sure her kids had all the resources they needed to feel supported. She took extra shifts at work to pay for her daughter's camp and found a great therapist for her son.

Affirmation

*I will be compassionate with myself for
the decisions I've made.*

Doubt

"Maybe if we give marital counseling one more try, we can save our marriage."

Doubting or second-guessing is common in the early days of separation and divorce. You may find that you doubt yourself or the decisions your spouse is making. Looking back, you may rehash what happened, trying to understand where things went wrong. Many women believe that greater understanding will lead to a change in the outcome. If your spouse made the decision to leave, you may try to repair the damage to your marriage and end the pain you're in. It's not unusual to wonder if your marriage would have survived if you'd just communicated better, earned more money, looked younger, or had more sex.

If you initiated the divorce, there may be moments when you doubt your decision. You may wonder if all the pain of separation and divorce is worth it. Divorce will be painful, but that doesn't mean it's not the right decision for you. You will feel better eventually, but in the short term, the rollercoaster of feelings is inevitable.

> Only a month after Gina and Anthony's wedding, Anthony became emotionally abusive and controlling. Following every one of his angry outbursts, he apologized and laid on the charm with dinners out and Gina's favorite flowers. As time passed, Anthony became angrier and more threatening. When Gina finally told him she could no longer live with his rage, she was terrified of his reaction. Instead of blowing up like she expected, he apologized for his behavior and promised to become a better husband. Anthony's "apology tour" was convincing. Gina began to doubt herself. Maybe her expectations of marriage were too high? Maybe he would change? She really didn't want to go through a divorce, so she reconsidered her decision. Four days later, Gina came home late from a busy shift at work. Anthony was waiting for her on the front porch and berated her all night long. In the morning, she knew she had to trust her initial decision.

Affirmation
*I may never reach 100 percent certainty, but
I am certain enough to move forward.*

Sadness

"I have never cried so much in my life."

Divorce is a profoundly sad life transition, one that no one dreams of when they get married. Feeling sad is a normal reaction to loss and can take many forms. Maybe you cry at the drop of a hat, feel hopeless or exhausted. You may find it difficult to picture a bright future. Many women experience decreased energy levels, and don't feel up to their usual activities. It's important to distinguish between feeling *sad*, which is a common, appropriate reaction to divorce, and feeling *depressed*, which is a more complex condition that may warrant support from a mental health professional.

Please don't hesitate to contact your doctor if you have lost interest and pleasure in most activities, have significant changes in your appetite or sleep, feel particularly fatigued or low-energy, have difficulty concentrating, or feel hopeless or suicidal. These may be signs of depression, and your doctor can provide options to help you feel better. You can also find additional ways to get support in the Resources section at the end of the book.

> Angel and Booker were married for forty years. Now retired, they looked forward to spending more time with their grandchildren. They had survived many tragedies during their marriage, including the death of their first child. Angel had supported Booker through his gambling addiction and was dependent on him both financially and emotionally. When she learned he'd lost over $100,000 in one weekend and that

they'd need to sell their house, she was devastated. She loved Booker, but the betrayal was too great for her to overcome and she knew she had to end the marriage. She had spent too many years helping him fight his addiction. Angel went from feeling sad and hopeless, crying all day long, to feeling suicidal and depressed several months later. Fortunately, she had a good relationship with her doctor, who prescribed antidepressants and referred her to a therapist. Angel also had a strong connection to her church and opened up to her pastor about her situation. Slowly, she regained stability as her mental health improved.

Affirmation

Losing my marriage is heartbreaking, but I know this feeling won't last forever.

Anger

"I'm so mad I feel like my head is going to explode."

Many women feel annoyed, irritated, frustrated, angry, exasperated, and even rageful during their divorce. You may experience intense dislike or hatred toward your spouse, especially if you've been betrayed or abused, or if your ex is fighting with you about parenting plans or asset division. As women, we're taught to repress our anger, but anger is a valid emotion that can be a powerful fuel for action. It's important to determine if you're feeling pure anger or if your anger is masking another feeling that's harder to express. You may find it easier to be angry than to express some of the more vulnerable feelings right beneath the surface: hurt, betrayal, disappointment, and rejection.

Anger can manifest physically as increased heart rate and blood pressure, sweating, digestive issues, muscle tension, and difficulty sleeping. While it's perfectly normal to feel angry during a divorce, be careful not to act on your anger in ways that will hurt you or someone else. Long-term anger can be unproductive, exhausting, and destructive. Finding ways to process your emotions will help you avoid becoming bitter in the long term. Using your anger as a catalyst for change can be transformative. After all, living well is the best revenge.

> Twenty-seven years into their marriage, Carolina discovered that Theodore had had an affair with his assistant while Carolina was recovering from breast cancer. Theodore had not been supportive through her surgery, chemotherapy, and radiation, but Carolina assumed he was preoccupied with work. When she learned it was because he was having an affair, she was enraged. She had trouble sleeping and could barely eat. When a co-worker asked her why she was so angry, she realized she needed help to process her rage toward her husband. Otherwise, her feelings would leak into her other relationships and create further damage. Once she began processing her emotions, she realized she was feeling not only angry, but also betrayed, neglected, and rejected, feelings that had been much harder to acknowledge.

Affirmation

My anger is valid and I have every right to express it in healthy ways.

Loneliness

"I'm fine during the week, when I'm working, but the weekends are really hard."

Loneliness is an internal experience rather than a reflection of how many other people are around. You can be lonely in a crowd, or in a marriage. Or you can be perfectly content spending time alone. Divorce is often a lonely experience, as you've lost the person you spent so much of your life with. Many women miss the little conversations of daily life—"The plumber didn't call back," "Joey got a B-plus on his math test," "Do you think we need more eggs?"—interactions they had with a spouse that don't feel important enough to tell a friend. What's more, other people who haven't been divorced may not understand your experience, which can feel isolating.

> Sandra and Dwayne didn't have big arguments, but they bickered constantly. Every interaction became a power struggle. When Dwayne moved out, Sandra was shocked. She thought they'd just keep bickering until they died. With their kids out of the house and Dwayne gone, the house was eerily quiet. Although Sandra found the bickering to be unpleas-

> ant, she was used to it, and the absence was a challenge for her. Weekends were especially hard as she felt adrift without Dwayne there. They had lost a lot of friends over the years due to the constant conflict between them. Finally, Sandra decided she needed some new friends, and she threw herself into volunteering at organizations that mattered to her. Soon her weekends were full again, spending time with new friends volunteering at work that made her feel valuable.

Affirmation

*I'm okay on my own. I am
learning to be independent.*

Fear

"Every time I see an email from my attorney, my heart starts racing."

Fear is a short-term, high-alert emotion that can cause increased heart rate, sleep difficulties, sweating, and nausea. Going through a divorce means living with a lot of uncertainty, which can be frightening. It's normal to feel afraid if your spouse is acting unpredictably or in ways that are financially, emotionally, or physically harmful to you. Some women feel a sense of terror about the thought of being alone or the unknown that awaits them. Others have panic attacks, either for the first time or that return from a previous era of their lives.

> Faith left Gerard after twenty-two years of marriage. Gerard had been an absent parent and a bully during their marriage. He told Faith that if they divorced he would fight for full custody of the kids. This was her worst fear, and he knew exactly how to take advantage of that. When Faith finally told him she was leaving, Gerard threatened her repeatedly. She moved into an apartment across town with her kids but lived in fear for the first year. She worried Gerard would somehow end up with full custody, even though she was the primary parent and he had only minimal contact with their kids. Whenever Faith saw an email from him, her heart raced, and her palms got sweaty. Finally, she arranged for emails from her ex to automatically forward to her sister, who then summarized them for her. Her lawyer reassured her repeatedly that there was no legal justification for Gerard to get custody, but Faith couldn't let go of the fear until the divorce was finalized.

Affirmation

I can be afraid and courageous at the same time.

Regret

"I can't believe I missed so many red flags."

Regret means wishing you'd made a different decision in the past because of consequences you're facing in the present. You can feel regret over things you did do *or* things you didn't do. Many women experience regret *about their marriage* during the divorce process.

Regret can take many forms, including:

- Wondering if you did enough to save the marriage
- Blaming yourself for not leaving sooner or ignoring red flags
- Feeling angry at yourself for choices you made during the marriage
- Wanting to take back the decision to give up or scale back your career
- Wishing you had been more involved with the finances during your marriage
- Feeling sad about how much unnecessary conflict there was
- Wondering if getting married to your spouse was a mistake

While regret is often an uncomfortable emotion, it can also act as a powerful reminder to reflect, grow, and change.

> Libby and Chloe were married for twelve years when Libby decided she wanted a divorce. During their marriage, Libby left her lucrative job in technology to stay home with their three kids. She was in charge of their house and children, while Chloe took care of the finances. Libby had no idea how much Chloe had mismanaged their finances until their car was repossessed in their driveway. When Libby eventually uncovered

> the web of financial lies and deceit, she blamed herself for not paying closer attention to their finances. She regretted that she had not been more involved. Looking back, she could see all the red flags she had ignored. She vowed that in her next relationship, she would never give up so much financial control.

Affirmation

*I did the best I could with
what I knew at the time.*

Anxiety

"How will I ever afford to live on my own?"

Anxiety is characterized by worried thoughts and physical symptoms that trigger the body's stress response. Many women worry about their future, their financial well-being, their children, and their own mental health during a divorce. The Holmes-Rahe Stress Scale ranks divorce as the second most stressful life event, second only to death of a spouse.

If you find yourself feeling anxious, make a list of things that are in your control versus out of your control. Then try to focus your energy on the things you can control.

> Elise and Frank gradually fell out of love with each other after thirty-five years of marriage. Elise was outgoing and loved

adventure, while Frank was an introvert who enjoyed tinkering with projects in the basement. With the kids grown up and out of the house, they no longer had any shared interests. Elise tried to strike up conversations, but Frank didn't want to engage. After many years of living separate lives in the same house, Elise finally decided she wanted a divorce. Her primary anxiety was more financial than emotional, and she worried constantly about losing the house she loved. She felt anxious about how she'd afford her monthly expenses and healthcare costs when she got older. Elise met with a financial planner who helped her see that if she got a part-time job and trimmed her expenses, she could stay in the home she loved.

Affirmation
I am strong and can handle
whatever comes my way.

Overwhelm

"I feel like I'm drowning."

Feeling overwhelmed happens when our lives are moving faster than our nervous systems can handle. I often tell the women in my support groups that getting divorced is like having a really horrible part-time job in addition to your already busy life. Worse than working for free, you have to pay to do this job! There are no paid sick days, no scheduled vacation days, and your boss is awful. The hours are unpredictable, and every task takes longer than it should. The good news? Divorce is not your forever job. You will move on. In the meantime, you need to schedule your own sick days and vacation days, as you are the only one looking out for your needs. When you feel overwhelmed, the solution is not to work harder, but instead to take scheduled breaks so you can work smarter.

The legal and financial aspects of divorce are basically one big business deal. Unfortunately, we know that when stress increases, cognitive functioning decreases. This is why it may feel more challenging to concentrate, read, and understand financial and legal terms right now. Don't worry, your brain will return to its regular state, but for now, take it slow and give yourself time to integrate all this new information. Be patient and compassionate as you take one step at a time, and be sure to schedule breaks for yourself.

> Tina was a nurse with three young kids when her husband, Steve, left her. Steve moved across the country, and Tina was left to single-parent with a busy full-time job. By the time she got home after work, fed and bathed her kids, and put them to bed, she was exhausted. She couldn't find the time to do anything else—life had gotten overwhelming. Her attorney kept asking her to complete her financial paperwork, but she felt too burdened by her job and parenting to get it done. Finally, sensing Tina was going to break down, her sister came for a weeklong visit. When Tina went to work, her sister did her laundry and grocery shopping. When Tina got home, her sister fed and

> bathed the kids so she could focus on her paperwork. After a week of working just an hour a night, Tina was in much better shape to meet with her attorney with her completed financial forms. Tina nicknamed her sister "my guardian angel."

Affirmation
*I will tackle one task at a time
and ask for help when I need it.*

Shame

"I feel like a failure."

While guilt is the feeling that you've *done* something bad, shame is the feeling that you *are* bad. You may feel like a failure, that you should have made your marriage work regardless of the circumstances. Many women feel unlovable or worthless when their marriage ends. I'm struck by the level of shame the women in my practice feel even if their spouses were the ones who cheated, struggled with addiction, or were controlling or abusive. As a society, we still place the responsibility of caring for and maintaining an intact family on women. Labeling your divorce or yourself as a failure is not accurate and won't serve you or anyone else. If you're experiencing shame, find ways to acknowledge it, talk about it, practice self-compassion, and challenge your thoughts. Rather than feeling like you're a failure or your marriage was a failure, see if you can adopt one of these narratives instead:

- "We will be better co-parents than romantic partners."

- "We were a good match in the beginning, but we both changed."

- "We tried valiantly to save our marriage."

- "Our marriage didn't last, but I learned a lot from it."

> Anya and Tom married just a year after they met. Soon after, Anya realized how mismatched they were, but she'd grown up attending a Catholic church listening to sermons that were vehemently opposed to divorce. Anya tried for years to make her marriage work, giving up more and more parts of herself that didn't match Tom's strict code of behavior. She quit her job and gave up her friends to try to please Tom, but in the end, she felt she had to save herself instead of her marriage. Most of her family and friends disapproved of her choice, increasing her sense of shame. In her first therapy appointment, she told her therapist that she was a "broken, unlovable failure." It took time for her to understand where her shame came from and how to cope with it. She worked with the therapist to come up with a new, more compassionate way of understanding her marriage and her decision to divorce.

Affirmation

*Just because my marriage ended
does not make me a failure.*

Relief

"I feel like I can breathe again."

As tension leaves your body and you begin to feel safer, you'll likely experience relief. You may even notice you can breathe easier. If you were the one to initiate your divorce, it may feel like a huge weight has been lifted. You've probably been thinking about ending your marriage for some time, so finally telling your spouse means no longer living with the unspoken knowledge that you're planning an exit.

Many women feel relieved that they are no longer living in an unworkable marriage. Less fighting, tension, and criticism means a greater sense of calm and peace. Try to lean in to your feelings of relief any time you feel them, as they'll be a welcome respite from more challenging emotions. Most people who are divorcing are coming out of unhappy marriages, and the relief of no longer living with painful arguments and tension can be palpable.

> Jodi and Juan had four children and fought constantly about how to parent them. Jodi wanted the kids to follow house rules and have consequences for their behavior, while Juan had a more relaxed parenting style. Despite years of marital counseling, they were unable to resolve their differences, and the fighting continued. Jodi was living in a constant state of tension and found parenting much easier when Juan wasn't around. Once they separated, Jodi felt a level of relief she hadn't expected. She was sad and angry as well, which she'd predicted, but she was surprised by how relieved she felt.

> Even with four kids, parenting was calmer and more peaceful without Juan's interference. It felt easier to be a single parent than a fighting co-parent. Jodi's kids settled in quickly, and she was relieved to see they seemed happier as well.

Affirmation

*I am letting go of tension and
conflict as I lean in to relief.*

Grieving the Loss of the Marriage

Often referred to as an ambiguous loss, the end of a marriage may look and feel similar to losing a loved one to death. Divorce signals the death of a marriage, and while your former spouse will remain living, the relationship you once had will be changed forever. Processing the end of your marriage and all the associated losses is a vital part of your healing journey.

When a married person dies, friends and family gather to support their grieving spouse. We have well-developed traditions in place that provide immediate community and emotional support for those who are grieving. Loved ones gather for the funeral, send flowers, and bring lasagnas. No one blames, stigmatizes, or questions the grieving widow. We need to start doing the same for people when their marriage ends. Divorce, like death, is a major life transition that should be treated with compassion and care rather than judgment and avoidance. The next time you have a friend who's navigating a divorce, bring her a baked lasagna and a bouquet of flowers. She deserves it. And so do you.

There are many similarities between grieving widows and women navigating divorce. Both groups report feeling sad, lonely, overwhelmed, worried, upset, angry, and confused. Many widows experience a sense of relief when their spouse dies, especially if the death follows a long illness. Likewise, many divorced women are relieved when the legal process gets finalized, even when the divorce was not their choice.

The one major area where divorced women and widows' feelings tend to differ is shame. It's much more common for women going through divorce to feel shame and stigma. We have lasting traditions and lucrative businesses that support the wedding industry. Getting and staying married is still considered a worthy and valued goal in our society, *even when the marriage is unhealthy*.

Ending a marriage can feel like a personal failure, something to be ashamed of, even when it's a necessary and healthy change. Our society has yet to develop communal traditions to support people navigating divorce, even though nearly half of marriages end in divorce. We need to keep speaking up in authentic ways about divorce and change the language and attitudes around it. I look forward to the time we view the end of a marriage as a life transition or a family restructuring rather than a stigmatizing event.

Many of the women in my support groups celebrate the finalization of their divorce with a party, a special trip, or the purchase of a new piece of jewelry. In the last few years, divorce registries have become more common and offer a way for people to receive support like they would if they were getting married or having a baby. Check out Fresh Starts Registry if you want to create a registry of your own.

Hidden Losses

Like a grieving widow, you may be overwhelmed by feelings of loss as you navigate your divorce. Many women have already experienced losses (of identity, self-esteem, and physical touch, for example) during their marriage. As you grieve your marriage, you may also reexperience the grief of past deaths, breakups, or emotional wounds. Right now, losses may be all you can see. In time, they'll begin to feel less intense, and you'll come to recognize some of the positive outcomes of this transition that you couldn't see before.

There are obvious losses that go along with divorce: a loving relationship with your spouse, the family home, and financial security, for example. But you may find more subtle losses arise as well, ones that your friends and family may not fully appreciate.

Time with Your Kids

When faced with so much grief, losing time with your children can be devastating at first. You may feel lonely and sad or worry about them when they aren't with you. Gradually, you'll adjust to your new parenting schedule and may even welcome the alone time. Shared parenting can give you a chance to recharge during your non-parenting time and be more present when your children return home.

> Greta dreaded Saturday nights when she first separated from Sheila. She grocery shopped and cleaned during the day when her kids were with their other mother, but Saturday nights were the worst. She missed her kids and was lonely with-

out them. She didn't feel up to socializing with her married friends, and she couldn't bear to go out to eat by herself. After the first six months passed and she began to heal from the pain of her divorce, however, she looked forward to her Saturday nights. She joined a Saturday afternoon softball league and started a book club with other divorced women she met online. While she still missed her kids when they weren't with her, over time she began enjoying these nights to herself.

Mutual Friends

It can be challenging for friends to remain close with both members of a divorcing couple. Some may choose your spouse, and others may prioritize spending time with other couples. This tends to be very painful and will reveal a lot about who is and isn't there for you. Divorce can also offer an opportunity to make new friends—other divorced women are great candidates. Be sure to clearly communicate with your friends what you need from them. If it's helpful to make weekend plans because those days are hardest for you, let them know. If you need support with childcare, give them a heads-up. They may also appreciate guidance on how to treat your ex. For instance, is it okay to invite both of you to the same party, or do you need no contact right now? Clear communication is key!

Lorna and Greg were part of a large group of friends they'd known since college. When they first separated, their friends

> tried to stay neutral and remain close with both of them. Lorna felt okay about this until Greg started dating just a month after moving out. After that, Lorna found it increasingly difficult to maintain relationships with their mutual friends. Gradually, the group divided into the "Lorna camp" and the "Greg camp." Lorna's friends supported her through the divorce and looked to her for guidance on whether she wanted information about Greg's dating life. Lorna was sad to lose the friends who supported Greg and felt surprised by how many of her relationships shifted after the divorce.

Traditions

Perhaps you were a family who always dressed up for Halloween together—adults included—or a family who went skiing on New Year's Day with your spouse's family. Maybe you and the neighbors had a pumpkin pie contest every Thanksgiving and your spouse was one of the judges. Whatever your traditions were, chances are some of them will change with the divorce. While some families keep certain customs after a divorce, most develop new ones as well. I encourage you to be proactive about creating new traditions and involve your children in that process.

> Every year, Layla and Ed had Thanksgiving with Ed's extended family. After they divorced, Layla was at a loss when that first holiday season came around. Because she was still reeling from the divorce, she decided her kids should go with

> Ed to his family's Thanksgiving. She didn't want to be alone, so she decided to volunteer at a domestic violence shelter. The mood at the shelter was festive, and everyone worked hard to deliver a delicious feast for the residents. The time passed quickly, and Layla felt useful and included. In fact, she enjoyed that day so much that she decided she'd bring her kids the next year. They loved it, too, and decided to make volunteering their new Thanksgiving tradition.

In-Laws

Some women are relieved to give up their in-laws. But others have developed rewarding relationships with their spouse's family over many years and feel heartbroken to lose those connections. It's not written in stone that relationships with in-laws will change, but even in the best cases, there's often loss involved. Either the in-laws communicate less frequently, or the relationship becomes superficial or strained. If you lose contact with your in-laws, it's likely your spouse has only delivered one side of the story. This can be a painful reality to come to terms with, but part of healing is accepting that you can't control your ex's narrative about why your marriage ended.

> Alexa developed a close relationship with her three sisters-in-law over the twenty-five years she was married. When she divorced, she hoped they'd remain close. She was disappointed and hurt that two of them immediately sided with

> her husband and distanced themselves from her. The third sister, who'd also recently divorced, remained loyal to Alexa, but their relationship felt more forced. Alexa was relieved to maintain relationships with her young nieces and nephews, but she mourned the loss of closeness with the three sisters.

Identity

Many women love the role of wife and need to mourn that piece of their identity. Even more frequently, women mourn the status of being part of an intact family. This loss is most acute at the beginning of the divorce process, but can resurface at school events, holidays, and other special occasions for years to come. Although you may be losing this part of your identity, it's also a good opportunity to reflect on new ways of being in the world. Perhaps your divorce kept you isolated, but you're an outgoing person and want to nurture that part of yourself now. Maybe you let your hobbies and interests fall away when you were married but now have the time to reengage. There are endless possibilities for who you can become after your divorce.

> Edith and Harold were married for forty-five years when Harold had a near-fatal brain aneurysm. After he recovered, he abruptly decided to end their marriage. Edith was bereft. They had met as teenagers, married at age twenty, and raised six children together. Edith delighted in being a grandmother and loved gathering her extended family for Sunday dinners

> and holidays. She'd been a stay-at-home mother for most of her adult life and loved her roles as wife, mother, and grandmother. When Harold left, she grieved the loss of their marriage but even more intensely, her role as wife. Her daughters helped her see that despite losing that part of her identity, she would always remain a mother and a grandmother.

Vision of Your Future

When you were married, you probably envisioned what your future would look like. Maybe you pictured finally working out the problems between you, traveling after retirement, or playing with your grandkids. Certainly, *this* is not what you imagined. Uncertainty about your future can be particularly difficult to accept when you're an established adult. But keep in mind that none of us can predict the future, and while it may feel daunting right now, this next stage of your life holds many possibilities.

> Joy and Ken struggled for years with infertility and finally decided to give up their dream of having kids. Instead, they both invested in their work and advanced in their careers. They made enough money to vacation in Italy every fall and talked about moving there when they retired. After discovering Ken had had an affair with a mutual friend, Joy decided to file for divorce. She mourned the loss of the marriage and the mutual friend. Particularly painful for her was the loss

> of their future plans together. She felt betrayed and adrift, unsure what her future would hold.

Physical Touch

Many women navigating divorce become acutely aware of the lack of touch in their lives. While some miss sex, too, most feel the absence of affectionate, nonsexual touch even more. They miss holding hands, a back rub, or snuggling in front of the TV. If you're suffering from a lack of touch and you can afford it, book a massage. In addition to providing relief and relaxation, massage has been shown to reduce stress, elevate mood, boost the immune system, and help with improved sleep. If massage is not for you, or out of reach financially, take any opportunity you can to hug a friend, snuggle a pet, or give yourself a foot rub.

> Tisha and Lamar divorced after Tisha discovered that Lamar was addicted to drugs and had secretly spent their life savings. Up until that discovery they'd had a very physically affectionate relationship. When Lamar moved out, Tisha's sister asked what she missed most about him. She replied, "I miss the physical presence of him. I felt safe sleeping in bed curled against him, and I felt comforted when he hugged me. Even when he was a jerk, I was still attracted to him." Tisha's sister suggested she adopt a dog, something Lamar had never wanted. Tisha was hesitant at first, but as soon as she brought her new dog home, they were inseparable. Her

> new pet couldn't replace the physical comfort Lamar had provided, but he offered a sense of safety and some much-needed snuggling time for Tisha.

Exercise: Identifying Feelings

Recognizing how you feel and why is one of the first steps in processing your emotions. Begin that important work by filling in the blanks below.

I feel shocked that

_____

_____

I feel guilty about

_____

_____

I doubt myself when

_____

_____

I feel sad because

_____

_____

I'm angry about

_____

_____

I feel lonely when

_____

_____

I'm afraid that

_____

_____

I regret that

_____

_____

I am anxious about

_____

_____

I feel overwhelmed by

_____

_____

I am ashamed of

_____

_____

I feel relieved that

_____

_____

Keep in mind that we're all capable of feeling many things at once. This phenomenon may be confusing, but it's natural to have mixed feelings. You may find that you are angry at your ex *and* sad about the loss, scared about your future *and* relieved the fighting has stopped, lonely on the weekends *and* too ashamed or exhausted to make plans. Anticipate that your feelings may be complex and messy right now.

By now, you know you'll *have a lot of feelings* during your divorce. But you may be thinking, "What am I supposed to *do with them*?" I'm glad you asked. In Chapter 6, we're going to talk about how to deal with all these emotions.

6

Hitting Your Stride

Now that we've identified the emotions you're likely to feel during your divorce, let's explore how to process them in healthy ways. Processing your feelings requires that you let yourself experience them fully. Only then will you be able to release them. To do that, I recommend joining a support group, writing in a journal, or talking to a therapist or friend.

You've got to feel it to heal it.

Writing your feelings down or saying them out loud helps you organize, externalize, and validate those emotions. Some of the benefits of this kind of processing include:

- Increasing your emotional vocabulary so your feelings are less confusing

- Reducing the emotional intensity of your feelings so they're less overwhelming

- Releasing or letting go of feelings

- Allowing yourself to experience feelings without acting on them

- Paying attention to the ways feelings show up in your body

- Improving your self-awareness

- Deepening your relationships as you open up and share your vulnerable feelings with people you trust

- Developing a greater sense of empathy for others

Emotions are like waves. If you let them happen, they'll move through you naturally. Like waves, you can't stop them from coming, but you can allow them to wash over you. Because feelings are persistent, they won't simply go away if you deny them. Avoiding emotions by overusing alcohol, drugs, sex, or food, by working or exercising too much, or by shutting down will inevitably slow down your recovery. Suppressed feelings can start to manifest in unhealthy ways, including:

- Taking anger out on an innocent person/animal/object (yelling at people who don't deserve it, treating a pet harshly, breaking things in frustration)

- Extreme irritability (road rage, overreacting to small inconveniences, viewing everything through a negative lens)

- Out-of-control or self-harming behaviors (physically harming yourself, excessive drinking or drug use, driving too fast, risky sex, or other dangerous behaviors)

- New or increased physical pains or illness (stomachaches, headaches, back pain, dizziness, joint pain, skin problems, heart trouble)

- Becoming a harsh critic of your feelings (denying, judging, or criticizing them; saying things like "I shouldn't feel this way," "I'm probably overreacting," "I'm such a loser for feeling this way," or "I refuse to feel sad")

- Isolating yourself in order to avoid talking about your situation (trying to go it alone or handle it all by yourself)

Six Steps to Processing Your Emotions

> *I sat with my anger long enough until she told me her real name was grief.*
>
> **C. S. Lewis**

People process their feelings in different ways, and it's important to find what works for you. Here are six steps for processing that may help you identify, accept, and let go of your emotions.

1. Recognize how you're feeling

You're going to feel a lot during this time, so face your emotions head-on. It's valid and appropriate to have many feelings during a divorce. Know they are there for a reason. As you process, try to distinguish between thoughts and feelings. "I feel anxious about how I'm going to afford my rent" is a *feeling* whereas "I'm not going to be able to pay my rent and I'm going to have to move" is a *thought*. "I'm sad I'm not going to see my kids every day" is a *feeling*. "My kids are going to hate living in two homes" is a *thought*.

2. Label your feelings

Get specific about how you're feeling. Are you sad, lonely, or devastated? Frustrated, irritable, resentful, angry, or enraged? Each feeling word has a different meaning. It's useful to get specific about your emotions as that can guide how you choose to act on them. For example, if you're feeling *frustrated* about a text you received from your ex, you might decide to call a friend to vent or write about it in your journal. On the other hand, if your ex sends you a text that *enrages* you, you may want to cry, scream as loudly as you can, or channel your rage into an intense workout.

3. Accept how you're feeling

Accepting waves of emotion as they come is important. Ignoring, criticizing, minimizing, or judging them won't help you process them, and will likely make you feel worse. Feelings aren't right or wrong; they just exist. You already feel angry, but feeling ashamed that you feel angry just adds unnecessary baggage to an already difficult time. Make a commitment to yourself that you'll accept any emotions that arise without judgment. Remember, emotions are not your enemy, and they won't last forever if you do the work of processing them.

4. Get curious about your feelings

Once you've recognized, labeled, and accepted your feelings, start to get curious about them. Where did they come from? What are they trying to tell you? Do they have a history? When have you felt this way before? Do you have unprocessed feelings from the past that make the current ones seem even more intense? Are they showing up in your body as well?

5. Soothe yourself

After you've labeled and expressed how you feel, you can figure out how to soothe yourself so the feelings are less intense. Crying, journaling, breathing, exercising, listening to music, humming, meditating, mindfulness exercises, and talking are just some of the ways that people soothe themselves.

6. Learn from them

Your feelings are an important form of communication. Does your anger communicate that you need to strengthen or enforce your boundaries? Does your sorrow teach you that you need to reach out for more support? Does your fear tell you that you need to be more proactive about getting informed? Use your emotional state to motivate you and teach you important lessons.

> *Feeling all your feelings is hard, but that's what they're for. Feelings are for feeling. All of them. Even the hard ones.*
>
> **Glennon Doyle**

Three Simple Ways to Soothe Yourself

Here are three things to do when your emotions feel overwhelming. They're all easy to learn and can be done in less than a minute. If you think you might need a reminder, bookmark this page for later.

1. Box Breath

Box breath is a simple, fast way to reduce stress and calm down. Used by the military, athletes, and first responders to focus and gain control, box breath can also slow your heart rate. Practice box breath when you're feeling relaxed so you're already familiar with it when you feel anxious or overwhelmed. When you get into bed at night, box breath can help you decompress after a long day and calm your thoughts so you fall asleep more easily. It's also a great practice if you are dreading an exchange with your ex and need to feel calmer.

- Breathe in through your nose while slowly counting to four. Notice how it feels as the air enters your lungs.

- Hold your breath for four seconds without inhaling or exhaling.

- Exhale slowly through your mouth for four seconds.

- Hold your breath for four seconds without inhaling or exhaling.

- Repeat.

2. The 5-4-3-2-1 Mindfulness Exercise

This is another easy, quick exercise you can do anytime and anywhere when you feel overwhelmed. Stop whatever else you're doing for a minute. Take a few deep breaths.

- Look around and identify **five things you can see**, paying attention to color, shape, and texture. This might be a lamp, the sky, your shoes, or anything else in your environment.

- Then identify **four things you can touch**, focusing on their texture, weight, and temperature. Maybe you feel your feet touching the ground, your shirt touching your neck, your hand on the desk.

- Next identify **three things you can hear**. Maybe it's the buzzing of the air conditioner, music in the distance, or the breeze outside.

- Then identify **two things you can smell**. Maybe it's the scent of hot pavement, flowers on your table, or your dog's breath.

- And finally, identify **one thing you can taste**. Maybe it's the remnants of the last thing you ate or your morning toothpaste.

As you identify each of these sensations, you'll notice that you feel calmer and more peaceful. Don't worry if you can't identify them all. This is a time for grace, not perfection. It's ideal if you can practice this exercise every day, but even doing it a few times when you feel stressed will benefit you.

3. Humming

Believe it or not, humming is an excellent way to relieve stress. While it may sound silly, humming can promote multiple mental and physical health benefits, including lower blood pressure and heart rate, increased oxygen and melatonin, and improved mood and sleep.

Humming also stimulates the vagus nerve, which is part of the parasympathetic nervous system that calms digestion, respiration, and heart rate. You can pick a song you like or just hum your own tune. Go ahead and try it!

The Power of Positive Affirmations

In addition to overwhelming emotions, you may find yourself flooded with negative thoughts about yourself, your situation, or the world. Affirmations are short, positive statements that challenge negative thoughts and replace them with more hopeful, empowering ones. They serve as reminders of your strength and resilience and help you to shift your focus away from negativity. In fact, the repetition of positive affirmations can rewire your brain by activating neural pathways and changing the way you think. Repeating an affirmation allows you to practice self-compassion at a time when you need it most.

Affirmations are even more effective when paired with an action, preferably something you do several times a day. For instance, you can repeat your affirmation every time you get in your car, enter your house, or brush your teeth.

Exercise: Write Your Own Positive Affirmations

You can use affirmations others have written (like the ones below) or create your own. What matters most is that they fit your unique emotional landscape.

Read the affirmations below and check the ones that speak to you. When you're done with the list, try writing some of your own.

- ☐ I will breathe through the shock of my situation. I am breathing in, I am breathing out.

- ☐ I may never reach 100 percent certainty, but I am certain enough to move forward.

- ☐ Losing my marriage is heartbreaking, but I know this feeling won't last forever.

- ☐ I did the best I could, based on what I knew at the time.

- ☐ My anger is valid, and I have a right to express it in healthy ways.

- ☐ I'm okay on my own. I am learning to be independent.

- ☐ I am strong and can handle whatever comes my way.

- ☐ I can be afraid and courageous at the same time.

- ☐ I will tackle one task at a time and ask for help when I need it.

- ☐ Just because my marriage ended does not make me a failure.

My Affirmations

_____

_____

_____

_____

Repeat your affirmations as often as possible each day. You can say them out loud or repeat them in your head. You get extra credit if you write them down and post them where you can see them.

Moving Too Quickly or Too Slowly? Find the Right Pace

The legal process of divorce often increases feelings of overwhelm and uncertainty. Unfortunately, the family court system isn't designed to consider how people are feeling. Instead, it's largely a way to get business done. The courts want to move couples through the divorce process quickly but are often so backlogged that the legalities drag on. Managing the stress of being in limbo can be very challenging. Not knowing what your parenting plan or finances will look like or if you'll have to change jobs or housing creates extra stress. This time of uncertainty will not last forever, but while you're in limbo, it may be helpful to concentrate on the things you *can* do. Many women intend to start exercising, eating healthier, and sleeping better *after* they get through the divorce. But I encourage you not to put off taking care of yourself—do as many of those things as possible *now*.

It can feel excruciating if the legal proceedings of your divorce move too quickly *or* too slowly. There are ways to change the pace, but you'll also have to accept that your ex and your respective legal teams will be moving at their own pace, too. This can introduce additional challenges to an already difficult process.

Moving Too Fast?

If your divorce wasn't your choice or started abruptly, it may be hard to catch up emotionally. You may feel panicked and unable to move forward with divorce-related tasks. Often, the initiating spouse wants to move along more quickly—move out, sell the house, divide the assets—while the non-initiating spouse is just trying to get through the day without an emotional breakdown. It's important to take time to gather information and recalibrate. Rushing into major financial, housing, and parenting decisions is not wise and won't serve you in the long run, especially if it's on someone else's timeline.

Many women facing divorce feel disempowered by their spouse's financial power, legal knowledge, and/or social status. If a significant power imbalance played a part during your marriage, expect that this will resurface in your divorce as well. Feelings of overwhelm or panic may force you into a stance of reactivity rather than proactivity. This may be especially true if you were blindsided or your divorce seemed to come out of nowhere. Keep in mind that your spouse will not be looking out for your needs. That is your job now, as unfamiliar as that may be for you. Slowing things down so you can fully understand what's happening is perfectly valid.

As you face legal negotiations, you may feel pressured to answer important financial and legal questions before you're ready. If you feel rushed, here are some strategies for empowering yourself and becoming more proactive:

- Take a few deep breaths as soon as you're confronted with a challenging topic. As you breathe in, you take in more oxygen and slow down your heart rate. Your mind will move from a state of panic to a more relaxed one.

- Respond rather than react. Reactions are immediate, without consideration of your long-term needs. Responses are thoughtful, planned ways of figuring out and communicating what you need.

- If your spouse's communications are upsetting or cause anxiety, don't answer right away unless the communication is time-sensitive in regard to your children. Agree that you'll each text each other "EMERGENCY" if there's a true emergency that needs immediate attention. Take the time you need to emotionally prepare to respond.

- Program your email to send all divorce-related messages into a special mailbox that you read only when you're ready.

- Use the phrase "I'll have to think about that and get back to you" as often as you like. This is especially useful if you're talking in front of your kids or if your spouse is bullying or rushing you into a decision. Give yourself time to think about your response.

Sophia Slows Things Down

Sophia was in a state of shock and disbelief when her husband, Clark, announced he wanted a divorce and would be moving out the next day. After thirty-four years of marriage, her brain couldn't compute that Clark was leaving so abruptly. For the first few weeks, she was sure Clark would realize what a big mistake he was making. When she woke up in the morning, her first thought was that she'd had a bad dream. After a few weeks, though, Sophia started to feel the emotional weight of Clark's decision. She couldn't eat or sleep, and she couldn't stop crying. Clark, on the other hand, was all business. He moved out as promised the very next day. Shortly thereafter, he told Sophia they should sell their house and divide up their assets. Because he had been the primary breadwinner, he proposed a division of assets that would benefit him, but felt sure Sophia would understand.

When Sophia first met with her therapist, she was panicked. She assumed that because Clark had filed for divorce and wanted to sell the house, she had to comply with his wishes. The therapist focused on helping her slow down the process. Sophia needed time to integrate this new information before making any major decisions. Just because Clark knew what he wanted didn't mean he could proceed without negotiations that included what Sophia wanted. The therapy focused on empowering Sophia to consult with her legal team and to figure out her needs and wants. Understandably, Sophia had a lot of overwhelming feelings, and she needed time to sort those out. Even though it frustrated Clark, Sophia slowed the process down and advocated for herself. She eventually bought him out of their house, stayed in the home she loved, and negotiated a 50-50 division of assets.

Moving Too Slow?

It would be reasonable to assume the person who initiates the divorce is the person who moves the legal and financial process forward. But over and over again, I've found that *the person who does the work in the divorce is the same person who did the work in the marriage.* In other words, the person who was primarily responsible for keeping the relationship/kids/house running will probably be the one who keeps the divorce progressing, *even if they didn't initiate it.*

People who are passive in their marriage tend to be passive in their divorce.

A divorce that moves too slowly can be frustrating and destabilizing as it keeps you connected to your ex and suspended in uncertainty. You may feel increasingly angry if your spouse was the one who initiated the divorce, but they refuse to move forward with the necessary legal tasks. If you were the one who initiated, you may feel impatient as you wait for your spouse to adjust to the news and start moving. While we cannot control other people (especially in a divorce), there are a few things you can do if your divorce is moving at a snail's pace and you're feeling stuck.

- Practice deep breathing every day. Know that the divorce will eventually be over. It's only a matter of time.

- Focus on self-care. Instead of waiting for the divorce to finish up *before* you exercise, eat better, drink less, clean your closets, or practice yoga, start some of those things now. In other words, focus on what you do have control over.

- There are many tasks in a divorce. If your spouse is holding one of them up and you're eager to keep moving ahead, focus on a different aspect of the divorce. For instance, if your spouse hasn't submitted the necessary financial documents, start working on your parenting plan or your new budget.

- If your spouse is financially motivated, remind them that it costs both of you when your lawyer has to reach out to their lawyer about an overdue task.

Carrie—Frustrated by the Slow Pace

Carrie and Naomi were married for eighteen years. Naomi was unhappy in the marriage for a long time as she felt Carrie didn't support her career as a professional actress. She told Carrie she wanted a divorce on July 4th weekend, but then refused to move out, get a lawyer, or talk about the impact the divorce would have on their kids. Carrie didn't want the divorce, but also accepted that Naomi had made up her mind. Anytime Carrie asked her about their next steps, Naomi told her she was working on it. Meanwhile, Naomi was taking expensive trips with friends, increasing their credit card debt. Finally, six months later, when Naomi still wouldn't address the divorce, Carrie felt she had no choice but to hire a lawyer. Naomi dragged her feet every step of the way, was late for every deadline, and refused every offer that was brought to the table for negotiation. Their divorce process was particularly frustrating to Carrie as she didn't want the divorce to begin with but ended up doing the bulk of the

> work to get it finalized. This was a familiar dynamic in their marriage as well.

What Does Progress Look Like?

What we think progress looks like   What progress actually looks like

Your emotional progress will not be linear. You may find yourself feeling better for a couple of hours or days until you wake up one morning and it's raining, and you can't stop crying. You may feel better for a few weeks and then get a distressing call from your lawyer, which sends you back into a state of panic. You get through the panic and begin to feel better but then see your ex at your kid's soccer game and they look happy. Or sad. Or they're friendly. Or distant. And you're devastated all over again. If you're the kind of person who stays very busy, you may find yourself feeling more when you slow down or try to fall asleep at night. When your feelings get intense again after a calmer period, this doesn't mean you're backsliding. Think back to the beginning of this process and remember how far you've come.

Many women in my support group lament that they haven't made any progress despite the time and money they've spent on the legal process. I like to remind them that divorce is both a legal *and* emotional journey, and despite the legal parts moving slowly, they've made enormous emotional strides. They have actively grieved, advocated for themselves, created new boundaries, and tried new things they never imagined possible. That counts as progress!

Permission to Do Less

Because this period is so challenging, it can be helpful to simplify your life. Completing the legal and financial steps of the divorce is time-consuming and emotionally exhausting. You may find you don't have as much time or energy to do the things you used to. Now is not the time to take on a new house project, accept more assignments at work, or start coaching your kid's soccer team. Instead, pare down responsibility, delegate tasks, and simplify. It's okay to eat cereal for dinner, wear the same outfit twice in one week, or go for your comfortable shoes rather than the fancier ones. Your house may be a bit messier, your emails a little tardier, and your meals a little less nutritious. And if that recipe you're making calls for fresh parsley and you don't have any in the house, you don't have to make a special trip to get it. *No one will blame you or judge you if you don't have parsley.* It's okay to let go of overfunctioning, give yourself a break, and do less.

Exercise: **Do Less!**

With the divorce underway and the rest of your life still expecting you to show up, your hands are bound to be very full. It's important to identify the areas in your life where you can ease up. I'm not suggesting you eat a peanut butter sandwich for every meal for a month, but can you be less of a gourmet cook? If you normally change your sheets once a week, can you make it once every ten days for a while? Try saying no to extra tasks and yes to offers of help.

Here are a few ideas to get you started:

- Simplify meal planning—it's okay to repeat your favorite (or easiest) dishes.

- Relax your cleaning regimen—maybe you don't have to vacuum quite as often.

- Reschedule unimportant meetings for sometime in the future.

- If your finances allow, hire someone to mow your lawn or shovel your driveway.

- Reduce your time on social media—set an automatic daily limit for yourself.

- Take a sabbatical from any committees or volunteer activities that don't bring you joy.

- Say YES when someone offers support.

What can you do to make your life easier for the next six months? Make a list here.

1. _____
   _____
   _____

2. _____
   _____
   _____

3. _____
   _____
   _____

4. _____
   _____
   _____

5. _____
   _____
   _____

Jada's Story

"Even though our marriage was crumbling, I didn't have the bandwidth to divorce him."

Jimmy and I met during our "party days" right after college. A mutual friend introduced us, and we hit it off pretty quickly. We spent a lot of our twenties drinking in bars and clubs with our friends. It was just part of the culture and never felt excessive back then.

The year I turned thirty, I unexpectedly got pregnant. Jimmy and I had been together for five years at that point, and we decided to get married before I started showing. I had a few glasses of champagne at our wedding, but other than that, I stopped drinking while I was pregnant. Jimmy didn't slow down, though, and for the first time, I noticed that his drinking was problematic. I was concerned, but didn't say anything, thinking he would cut back when the baby was born.

After the birth of our son, Jimmy drank even more. He didn't try to hide it on the weekends, but I caught him sneaking drinks during the week. I became a sleuth, smelling his breath when he got home, checking for empty bottles in his closet and the trunk of his car. I hated doing it, but I couldn't stop. Every time I caught him, he denied it or found some way to blame me.

All the lying made me feel crazy.

Discovering his lies and repeatedly confronting him was exhausting, so sometimes I just let it go. He had endless excuses. He told me he was drinking because we weren't having sex or because parenting was hard or because I wasn't fun anymore. I knew his job was stressful, so I hoped he would quit drinking, or at least cut down, when he got a new one.

He got his first DUI after he hit a tree, driving home late from a bar. When the officers arrived, they called an ambulance. Seeing him in the hospital, I had a huge rush of emotions. I was relieved he was alive but also so angry with him. I couldn't believe he would jeopardize our family like that. I was also flooded with anxiety. What if he was sent to jail? What if they took away his license? We couldn't afford a lawyer or a big fine. Most of all, I was worried he would keep drinking and his drinking would kill him.

He didn't end up going to jail, but he lost his license for three months and we had to pay a hefty fine. I was so resentful toward him that entire summer. Because he couldn't drive, I had to do all the errands, all the shopping, and all the daycare drop-offs and pick-ups. My life was already stressful enough, but when he got that first DUI, I almost lost my mind. I started drinking more, too. It seemed like a good way to relieve stress at the time, but it took a toll on my body. I thought about leaving him back then, but we had no money. I was under so much stress it was a miracle just to get through each day.

Even though our marriage was crumbling, I didn't have the bandwidth for a divorce.

His drinking got even worse when he couldn't drive. He used the excuse that if he wasn't driving, there was no harm in drinking at home. Most nights he ended up passed out on the couch.

I dreaded pulling into the driveway because I didn't know what I would find.

We only had sex once that year and I ended up getting pregnant again. Jimmy had his license back, he got a better job, and we had a little more money. He even stopped drinking for six months, which really helped. Our second son was an easy baby, and for a while, life seemed a little calmer and better. I felt like I had my husband back. Plus, with two kids, I knew it would be even harder to split up.

Life went on like this for another ten years with him drinking, going to AA meetings and sobering up for a few months, and then drinking again. Every time he went back to drinking, it got worse. He was a good enough parent when he was sober, but I hated seeing him drunk around the kids.

One of the hardest parts of my marriage was worrying about the impact on my kids.

The final straw came when Jimmy got a second DUI, this time with our kids in the car. I was so furious that when I got the call from jail, I picked up the kids but refused to bail him out. I called a divorce lawyer the next day.

Our divorce took a long time. We had major disagreements over custody of the kids. I wanted Jimmy to take a Breathalyzer when he had the kids, but he and his lawyers fought me on that. We couldn't agree on how much child support he owed me because he kept saying he wanted the kids 50 percent of the time. There was no way I was going to share custody, and I suspected he didn't really want the kids that much. During the course of our divorce, he fired two of his lawyers. That slowed the process down and cost us even more money. We drained our savings account just paying for the legal fees.

Sometimes I wanted to give up and just stay married because divorcing him was so stressful. But my best friend kept reminding me how much harder it was being married to him. She was right, of course, but it was still tough to remember.

Being in limbo, living with so much uncertainty for that long, was torture.

I knew we'd have to sell our house, but we couldn't until the divorce was final. He'd owe me child support, but not knowing how much made it really hard for me to budget. I wanted to keep the kids at their same school but wasn't sure if we could afford to stay in our town.

After two long years, we are finally divorced and the limbo is over. I bought a smaller house in the same town so my kids could stay at the school they love. The judge awarded me full custody. Jimmy sees the kids on the weekends, but never for overnights. I've had some great heart-to-hearts with my kids, who are teens now, about their father's drinking so they know what to look out for. So far, he's been sober when he's with them. My kids have adjusted well, and I feel so much better now that we're apart. I'm thankful I didn't give up on the divorce, because even though it was the hardest thing I've been through, in the end, it was worth it.

Can You Relate?

Put a check mark next to the sentences you relate to.

- ☐ All the lying made me feel crazy.
- ☐ Even though our marriage was crumbling, I didn't have the bandwidth for a divorce.
- ☐ I dreaded pulling into the driveway because I didn't know what I would find.
- ☐ One of the hardest parts of my marriage was worrying about the impact on my kids.
- ☐ Being in limbo, living with so much uncertainty for that long, was torture.

During a divorce, many things will be out of your control. Creating time for new opportunities and ways of being can help you feel more empowered. Examples of this include planning a vacation, taking a class, rearranging your bedroom, or getting a new haircut—whatever helps you feel like you're in the driver's seat of your own life.

Oona's Notes

- When your spouse hides or denies how much they are drinking on a regular basis, it's often a warning sign of addiction.

- Alcoholics often refuse to take responsibility for their actions. They blame others while excusing their own behavior.

- Al-Anon meetings (free meetings to support the loved ones of alcoholics) are an excellent resource if you're in a relationship with someone who has an addiction.

- Sometimes women spend so much energy coping with their unhealthy marriage that they don't have the mental energy to think about divorce.

- It's difficult to ride the hope/disappointment rollercoaster with a partner who's drinking excessively. If they are sober for a while, the disappointment when they start drinking again can feel even worse.

- Staying in an unhealthy marriage for many years can wear a person down, taking a big psychological and physical toll.

- Some judges will require a parent with documented addiction to take a Breathalyzer test (Soberlink is one example) during their parenting time.

> - Being in a suspended state of uncertainty—not knowing the future of your finances, custody, and housing—can lead to feelings of anxiety and overwhelm.

Exercise: **You're in Control**

Make two lists, one of things you can control right now and the other of things you can't. Here are a few examples to get you started.

Things You Can Control	**Things You Can't Control**
Being in the present moment	Knowing what the future holds
How you treat your kids	How your ex treats your kids
How you talk about your ex to your kids	How your ex talks to your kids about you
Your narrative of your marriage and divorce	Your ex's narrative of your marriage and divorce
Eating well, practicing good sleep habits	The physical impact of stress
Finding healthy ways to move your body	How your body responds to stress
Asking for support from others	Other people's needs

When you wake up each morning, look at your list and focus your energy on the things you can control.

Things I Can Control	Things I Can't Control
_____	_____
_____	_____
_____	_____
_____	_____
_____	_____

7

Preparing Children for the Journey Ahead

If you are a parent navigating divorce, I know you're concerned about your children. You might be wondering how they'll manage this complex transition, how you can best support them, and when to seek outside help. These are all important questions that will be explored in this chapter. In Chapter 8, we'll dive into parenting plans, co-parenting, and your children's transition to nesting or living in two homes. For guidance on how to tell your children you're getting divorced, see Chapter 4.

Parenthood is a journey, whether you are single, married, or divorced. There are ups and downs, successes and failures, and a lot of learning along the way. Remember that long before separation or divorce became a possibility, you supported your children through many milestones—some small, others more significant. Bringing your newborn home from the hospital, sleep training, introducing solid food, potty training, sending your child to kindergarten—you supported them as they adjusted to each developmental milestone. Divorce may be a bigger, more stressful transition, but it's a transition, nonetheless. You know your children better than anyone, and you already have the skills to help them navigate new situations. You can do this, even when it's hard.

It's not our job as parents to shield our children from challenging situations but rather to support them when they inevitably face difficult times.

In addition to your own loss and grief, you're bound to have feelings about your children's experience as well. Don't be surprised if you feel sad, anxious, and guilty as you navigate this journey with them. Your children will need you, as this will be a major transition for them, too. However, I cannot stress enough that you must put your own oxygen mask on first if you want to support your children. It's much harder to attend to your children's needs if you don't prioritize your own mental health and well-being.

What the Research Says

Stigma about divorce and its impact on children largely stems from research done during the 1970s, which indicated that divorce is psychologically damaging to children's well-being. However, over the next two decades, further research indicated that children with divorced parents showed similar social, emotional, and academic outcomes as children with married parents—as long as the parents were relatively cooperative and prioritized their children's needs.

Although children are adaptable and resilient, they still experience loss and grief during the divorce process and may exhibit temporary anxiety, depression, and stress. A 2013 *Scientific American* article "Is Divorce Bad for Children?" reviewed the research on how divorce impacts families and concluded that while children may experience negative effects in the short term, **"the vast majority of children endure divorce well."** As it turns out, divorce itself isn't what damages children's development long-term, but rather ongoing exposure to conflict, tension, or parental stress. Parents who relate to each other in a cold, dismissive way can be just as damaging to children's well-being as parents who have loud, aggressive arguments. Research over the past decade shows that reducing adult conflict in the home improves children's psychological well-being across all areas of development.

Children *can* adapt to divorce as long as parents attend to their needs and shield them from parental hostility and discord. In fact, many studies show that children with married parents who are chronically at war with each other have worse outcomes than children with amicably divorced parents.

It's also clear that parents play an important role when their children face challenges. In other words, the way parents respond to their children's stress has a significant impact. When parents prioritize their children's physical and mental health, their children tend to fare better long-term.

What This Means for Your Children

- Divorce will likely be stressful for them. They will experience loss and grief and may show temporary symptoms of stress.

- Your divorce is unlikely to permanently damage them. Their grief and stress will fade over time. Children are resilient and adaptable; they can recover from challenging situations.

- There are lots of ways you can support your children through divorce. Your love and thoughtful consideration of your children's needs matter. You're already your children's biggest supporter, and you have the capacity to help them through this time.

Many women stay in unhealthy marriages for as long as they can *for their children* but eventually decide they need to divorce *for their children*.

The Five Phases of Divorce Grief for Children

Just as you will proceed through the Five Phases of Divorce Grief, so will your children. Your divorce is an important transition for every member of your family. Their reactions to each phase will vary depending on the nature of the divorce, their age and temperament, and other factors. Like adults, they may move back and forth between phases or skip some altogether.

Heartbreak

The beginning of the divorce comes as a surprise for many children and can be heartbreaking. Even when children aren't surprised by this development, the reality is often difficult to face. The two people they rely on most are at odds with each other and distracted by stress and conflict. Separation and the possibility of having less time with each parent is bound to trigger waves of emotion. Losing their family home or moving into two homes can be temporarily destabilizing. It is normal and appropriate for children to feel sad, angry, and confused during this time. They might feel guilty, worry they have done something to cause this rift, and hope their parents will reconcile. Your job during this phase is to reassure your children that both parents love them, and the divorce is not their fault. Try to shield them from conflict as much as possible.

Supportive Language

- "We both love you and want you to know this isn't your fault."

- "Some things will change in our family, but the one thing that will never change is our love for you."

- "I can see how sad you are. This is a sad time, so it makes sense you're feeling that way. I want you to know we can talk about it anytime you want."

Rollercoaster

Children begin spending less time with each parent as their parents spend more time apart. They may absorb their parents' emotions and can feel neglected during this phase. As children transition to living in two homes, they may react with anger, confusion, and sadness. It's important to respond with consistency and open communication. Children need to know they can talk to you about their feelings without you getting defensive. Many children can't verbalize their feelings but communicate their emotions with behaviors. They may be more oppositional, clingy, or regressed—all ways to let you know how they are feeling. It'll be beneficial for them to get plenty of love, attention, and quality time with you.

Supportive Language

- "I know it's hard adjusting to having two homes. What can I do to make it easier?"

- "I can see how angry you are. This change is hard on all of us, and I know we're going to get through it."

- "I'm sorry I've been distracted this week. Let's plan some special time together this weekend."

Mending

In this phase, children are adjusting to their new schedules and routines. Their feelings about the divorce decrease in intensity and frequency. They are settling in, but still may experience waves of emotion at holidays, birthdays, and school events. With your children's help, you are deciding which old traditions to keep and which new ones to embrace. Your warmth and consistency will matter a lot during this phase. Your children may not talk about their divorce-related distress as much, so make sure you continue to check in with them.

Supportive Language

- "You've been a little quieter lately. Is anything on your mind about the divorce or anything else?"

- "Now that we've moved, we have options for trick-or-treating.

Do you think we should go back to the old neighborhood on Halloween or figure out who gives out the best candy in our new neighborhood?"

- "I know how hard it is that we won't be together on Thanksgiving this year. Let's think about a special meal we can have when you get back, and we'll have Thanksgiving here next year."

Letting Go

Your children have accepted that their parents aren't getting back together and are grateful there's less stress. They've fully settled into their schedule and routines. They're relieved to see you happier and have returned to focusing on their own lives again—as they should be! You can support your children now by working on your relationship with your co-parent, and doing everything in your control to be cooperative, flexible, and amicable, especially in front of your kids.

Supportive Language

- "Sounds like you had a great weekend. Did you go out to that yummy ice cream place you told me about again?"

- "I'm so proud of how you've handled all the changes in our family."

- "You left your cleats at practice? That's okay, I know you have a lot to keep track of with two houses. We can swing by after dinner and pick them up."

Moving On

You've moved on, your kids have moved on, and everyone is living their lives. Your children are engaged with school, friends, and activities and ideally have developed positive relationships with both parents. The divorce is no longer a constant concern but will always be part of their history. You may notice a less intense version of divorce grief when they're faced with significant life events like graduations and weddings. If you start dating, be thoughtful about how you share this news and introduce new partners. (See Chapter 10 for more on this topic.) Do your best to stay amicable with your co-parent and keep family events focused on your kids. If you and your co-parent are in constant conflict, it will be difficult for you or your children to reach this stage.

Supportive Language

- "I'm so excited for your graduation and so proud of you! I made a reservation at your favorite restaurant, and I've invited both sides of the family."

- "I wanted to let you know I'm planning to start dating again, but I want to assure you that I'll be taking it slow. We can talk about how you're feeling at any point."

- "Your aunt and uncle are getting divorced. I know you're close with your cousin. Maybe you could talk to her—you know, because you're a bit of an expert now."

Support Strategies from Infancy to Adulthood

Your children's reactions and your responses to them will vary considerably based on their ages and other factors. Understanding their needs will help you better support them. If you notice any changes in your children or are concerned about them, check in with your co-parent and ask what they're seeing. Children may react differently with each parent, which can provide clues about how to help them.

Infants

Even the youngest infants feel stress, too. They may become fussier, or experience changes in sleep and appetite. You may need to hold or rock them more often. (Rocking your baby can be calming for you, too.) Because babies develop so quickly anyway, it can be difficult to assess normal changes versus those related to divorce, but rest assured that these shifts are likely temporary.

When to seek help: Contact your child's pediatrician if your baby has significant changes in sleep or appetite or displays any other behaviors that concern you.

Toddlers

Very young children show stress primarily through behavioral regression and emotional instability. Perhaps your child was sleeping through the night and is now waking up several times. Maybe they had mastered drinking from a cup but are asking for a bottle again. They might express new fears or cry more than usual. Toddlers thrive on routine, so any changes in their environment may make them more prone to tantrums. These are all normal reactions to stress.

When to seek help: If your child's regression is significant and ongoing or their behaviors become dangerous or extreme, it's time to seek professional guidance. Your child's pediatrician can help you determine whether an intervention is needed or if your child's reaction is likely to pass.

School-Age Children

School-age children respond to stress in a variety of ways. Some can verbalize how they feel ("I feel sad/mad/afraid"), while others express their feelings with their behavior. They may have more difficulty sleeping, and you may notice more crying or irritability. School-age children may complain of headaches and stomachaches, or suddenly need more Band-Aids. It is important to let their teachers and guidance counselor know about changes to your family so they can keep an eye on them.

When to seek help: While many of these feelings are natural, it's important to seek help if they begin to impact your child's functioning. If your child refuses to go to school, develops new academic challenges, becomes socially withdrawn, or loses interest in activities they used to enjoy, seek guidance from their pediatrician, school guidance counselor, or child therapist.

Teenagers

Just like toddlers, teens change quickly and sometimes unpredictably. The good news is they tend to be more verbally expressive than younger children, but that doesn't mean they want to talk with you! You may also notice your teen acting more sad or irritable or seeming less interested in school. Their peers are important sources of support, so make sure you create opportunities for them to spend time with friends.

When to seek help: If your teen becomes significantly more sad, angry, or fearful, declines academically, or loses interest in friends or activities, talk with them about what you notice. Some teens engage in risky behaviors or abuse alcohol or drugs—all important red flags to keep an eye on. A counselor or therapist may be useful, but I don't recommend forcing teenagers to attend counseling against their will unless their behaviors are dangerous. Counseling is unlikely to be effective if they aren't open to it, and if they have a negative experience the first time, that could shape their feelings about seeking professional help in the future. If your teen turns down your first offer of counseling, mention it again in a few weeks or months so they know it's still an option. You can also see if there is another trusted adult—a relative, coach, or favorite teacher—they could talk to. In addition, speaking to their pediatrician or guidance counselor may be a helpful resource for both you and your teen.

Adult Children

Adult children will be affected by your divorce, too. Even fully grown children still need their parents to be parents. They may not want to know the details of the divorce or be your primary support—nor should they. Your adult children may worry about you being single and what will happen as you age. They may resist the idea of you dating again or be eager to see you in a new relationship. If they have children of their own, they may wonder what your divorce will mean for their children and family gatherings in the future.

When to seek help: Your adult children have their own lives now, so seeking help will be their decision. However, it's always a good idea to model good self-care, and you may want to share your coping strategies with them. Even if they decide not to pursue their own support, knowing that you are seeing a therapist (or going to yoga, a support group, or reading this book) will help them worry less about you.

What Children Need

Your children need a lot from you, whether you're married or navigating a divorce. Ideally, your kids will have two healthy, happy parents who prioritize and care about their interests. But even *one* healthy, happy parent can make a significant impact. This is true whether you are parenting solo or co-parenting with someone who doesn't focus on your children's needs. In addition to stable housing, food, and healthcare, children also need:

Love

Children need to feel loved and cared for, even when you're distracted or stressed. They want reassurance that their parents' love is not going to change, especially as they face such a big shift in their family structure.

- **Do** let them know the divorce isn't their fault and that your love for them will only grow.
- **Don't** hate your ex more than you love your children.

Peace

Children do best when they live in a home free from tension and conflict, especially conflict that relates to them. A peaceful, calm environment where the people they love get along helps them focus on their academic, social, and extracurricular activities.

- **Do** assume your children can pick up on nonverbal tension in the house.

- **Don't** have difficult or tense adult conversations in front of your children.

Connection

Children want to feel connected to their parents, caregivers, and other important adults in their lives. They need to know they belong to both sides of their family.

- **Do** support your children's relationship with their other parent and extended family.

- **Don't** make your children choose sides or cut off their access to your ex or your ex's family members (unless there's a safety issue).

Communication

Children thrive when the adults around them communicate well, model appropriate feelings, and are open and interested in what they have to say. Adult communication should stay between adults, and it's important for parents to avoid talking negatively about each other to or around their children.

- **Do** check in regularly about how they're feeling.

- **Don't** ask them to communicate with their other parent on your behalf.

Consistency

Children flourish in consistent, predictable environments. They *can* adapt to change (think: summer vacation) but do best when they have a steady, reliable schedule.

- **Do** keep them informed about your parenting schedule and any changes to it.
- **Don't** be regularly late for pick-ups and drop-offs with their other parent.

Expectations

Children need age-appropriate expectations. Whether it's setting the table for dinner or getting to school on time, these responsibilities help them feel competent and reliable. During a divorce, it's important to keep expectations kid-sized.

- **Do** provide reasonable, age-appropriate expectations.
- **Don't** expect them to fulfill all the duties your ex used to or lower your expectations because you feel guilty about the divorce.

Exercise: Parenting Checkup

Read the list of dos and don'ts below. Rate yourself on a scale of 1 to 5, with 1 meaning you need more work and 5 meaning you're doing great with this.

- **Do** let your child know the divorce is not their fault and that your love for them will only grow. 1 2 3 4 5

- **Don't** hate your ex more than you love your child. 1 2 3 4 5

- **Do** assume your child can pick up on nonverbal tension in the house. 1 2 3 4 5

- **Don't** have difficult or tense adult conversations in your child's presence. 1 2 3 4 5

- **Do** support your child's relationship with their other parent and extended family. 1 2 3 4 5

- **Don't** make your child choose sides or cut off their access to your ex or your ex's family members (unless there's a safety issue). 1 2 3 4 5

- **Do** check in regularly with your child about how they're feeling. 1 2 3 4 5

- **Don't** ask your child to communicate with their other parent on your behalf. 1 2 3 4 5

- **Do** keep your child informed about your parenting schedule and any changes to it. 1 2 3 4 5

- **Don't** be regularly late for pick-ups and drop-offs with their other parent. 1 2 3 4 5

- **Do** provide reasonable, age-appropriate expectations for your child. 1 2 3 4 5

- **Don't** expect your child to fulfill the duties your ex used to or lower your expectations because you feel guilty about the divorce. **1 2 3 4 5**

Give yourself credit for all the items you scored 4 or 5. Keep up the good work!

Offer yourself compassion and make a commitment to improve on all the items you scored 1, 2, or 3. You've got this!

Six Tips for Co-Parenting with an Uncooperative Ex

Managing your relationship with an unreliable or uncooperative co-parent can be very challenging, especially if you worry about your children spending time with them. I want to reassure you there is a lot of research supporting the fact that one healthy parent can outweigh the impact of an unhealthy parent. If you feel there are true safety concerns (this does not include less nutritious snacks or a later bedtime), it is important that you consult your legal team about options. Speaking with a child therapist or checking in with your child's pediatrician are other helpful avenues. If you don't have safety concerns but your relationship with your co-parent is strained or you're worried about their parenting style, here are six things that can help.

1. Check in with your co-parent about your concerns in a nonaccusatory tone. Use neutral starting phrases like "I know we both want what is best for Sammy" or "I know Sammy can exaggerate, so I wanted to check in about what he told me." Many chil-

dren aren't accurate reporters, and some will exaggerate to get attention. Before you react to what your child tells you, check in with your co-parent to hear their version of the story.

2. Establish firm, consistent boundaries with your ex. When you initially develop a parenting plan with your mediator or lawyer, make sure it's extremely detailed to limit ongoing negotiation as much as possible. For example, what happens if your child is too sick to go to school or there's a snow day? Anticipating these scenarios in advance, before you complete the legal part of your divorce, will help you avoid negotiations in the future.

3. Lean on technology to help. Many couples communicate over email or text to avoid testy verbal exchanges. Apps are available for creating parenting plan calendars and communication avenues. Communications are downloadable for use in court if necessary. One popular app, Our Family Wizard, even lets you know if the tone of your written communication is cooperative or not. Soberlink and other court-mandated alcohol-monitoring devices have helped countless co-parents monitor sobriety.

4. Use a third party. Many co-parents rely on a therapist, coach, or parenting coordinator to help them communicate effectively. Some mediators offer post-divorce "tune-ups." Unfortunately, many of these services are expensive, and both co-parents have to agree to use them, but in certain circumstances, they can be very supportive.

5. Keep your integrity intact. Don't allow your co-parent's nega-

tive behavior to influence your actions. Two wrongs never make a right. For example, your co-parent may be terrible at communicating important information about your child to you. You should still continue relaying updates to them, as that's what will benefit your child. Your co-parent won't help your child buy you a birthday card? Don't retaliate on their birthday. Instead, continue showing up with your values and modeling kindness and cooperation to your children.

6. Breathe in, breathe out, and accept that your child is going to have different rules and experiences in each household. There is very little you can do to influence your ex's parenting style. This can be a hard pill to swallow, but again, I want to reassure you that most kids learn to navigate different environments and are not negatively impacted by living in two homes with two sets of rules.

Helping your children through the divorce is one of the most important things you will do as a parent. Even though you and your spouse are divorcing, you'll always have a relationship if you have children together. A co-parenting relationship that is as amicable and functional as possible will benefit everyone. For further co-parenting information, see the Resources section at the end of the book.

When the "Best Interest of the Child" Is Not in Your Best Interest

During divorce, you'll hear the phrase "in the best interest of the child" a lot. This is a legal term that can be confusing. Of course, we all want to do what's in the best interest of our children, but parents have needs, too, and often those don't match up. When conflicts inevitably arise, it's crucial to find balance and compromise to achieve the optimal outcome for everyone.

As women, we're so accustomed to thinking about the best interest of our children (not to mention our spouses, bosses, and families) that it's often our default position. We tend to be less adept at thinking of our own best interest. Children thrive when their parents are happy, calm, and fulfilled. If you feel unsure about what legally qualifies as being "in the best interest of your children," be sure to consult with your legal advisor.

> Sadie had to pick up extra waitressing shifts when she got divorced. She had her kids 90 percent of the time, as her ex was largely absent, but he constantly threatened to take them. Her lawyer told her to make sure everything she did was "in the best interest of the children" to ensure she would get a fair custody agreement. She felt guilty about working long hours on Saturdays, but her kids didn't mind being at their grandmother's house while she worked. She needed money from the extra shifts to pay rent, and she also needed an occasional night out for her own mental health. Going out with her friends after work to unwind helped her feel more relaxed and present when she was with her kids. Sadie felt conflicted and worried she would be portrayed as neglectful by her ex, but her lawyer reassured her the court wouldn't penalize her for working or going out as long as her children were cared for.

If you find that your best interest and your child's best interest conflict, try these three things:

1. Talk to your child to understand how they feel and see if there is a compromise that works for both of you.

2. Consider the long-term impact of any decisions you make. You may feel conflicted about coming home from work an hour late today, but will you or your children remember it a month or year from now?

3. If you're still unsure what to do, consult with other parents or professionals to help you make the best choice.

Reflecting on your core values is a good way to approach these situations. Remember that by balancing self-care and caring for others, you are setting a model that will benefit both you and your children in the long term. Sometimes self-care looks like a night out with friends, while other times it looks like reevaluating where you invest your time and energy. For instance, women who stayed home with children during their marriage may need to return to paid work to support themselves after the divorce. Others choose to return to paid work for identity and self-esteem-related reasons. These choices, as well as continuing to stay at home, are all valid. Remember that the choices you make to care for yourself are ultimately choices to care for your children, too.

> Donna and Dave divorced when their kids were five, seven, and nine years old. Donna had been a stay-at-home mom,

while Dave worked long hours. As they negotiated their divorce, Donna decided to go back to work even though Dave's income was high enough to support the family. She loved her job before she became a mother and was eager to get back to working full-time. Additionally, she didn't want to be financially reliant on anyone. Dave was surprised and upset when she suggested they share parenting equally, as he had always counted on Donna for all their childcare needs. He tried to make Donna feel guilty about her return to work by bringing up "the best interest of the children." Donna then suggested that Dave work part-time so he could be more available to their children, which was also "in their best interest." Dave finally had to admit that they would both need to compromise and make changes to their schedules.

Now that we've addressed your emotional needs and the needs of your children during divorce, it's time to get into the details of parenting plans and co-parenting. In the next chapter, we'll review the pros and cons of various parenting plans, tips for smoother transition days, and information about sharing custody of the pets.

8

Finding Shelter: Transitioning from One House to Two

In this chapter we will discuss the pros and cons of various parenting plans, along with strategies to help your children adapt to living in two homes. First, a quick note on terminology. The terms "physical custody" and "legal custody" are increasingly considered outdated because of the way they imply ownership and control over children, yet many court systems still use them. I'll use the more current, child-centered terms "parenting time" and "decision-making responsibility" throughout this chapter. "Parenting time" (or "physical custody") refers to where the child lives, whereas "decision-making responsibility" (or "legal custody") refers to who makes the academic, health, dental, and religious decisions on behalf of the child.

Once you decide to separate or divorce, one of the first things to figure out is where everyone will live. Some couples live together for a while as they think through logistics or save up for one person to move out. Others move into separate homes right away. Separation involves many financial and emotional factors, and at first, your options may feel overwhelming and fraught. Of everything that happens during a divorce, making a change to your children's living situation (including where they live and with whom) will impact them the most. These decisions require thoughtful consideration.

If you need to live together for a period of time, it is helpful to come to an agreement about how you will interact with each other in front of your children. Some couples decide to spend less time in the house together and opt to create a parenting schedule that allows each parent regular time with the kids and regular time out of the house. Some couples move into separate bedrooms. Whatever you decide, know that your children will likely pick up on the tension between you, so make whatever schedule changes you can to reduce conflict and spend less time together.

Nesting Pros and Cons

Nesting, sometimes called bird nesting, is an arrangement where the children stay in the marital home and the parents take turns living there. Each parent lives with the children in the marital home on their parenting days but lives elsewhere on their non-parenting days. Some couples share a small apartment that they each use on their non-parenting time. Others find separate housing for their off days.

This arrangement can have many benefits for children. As they adjust to their parents' separation, their physical environment doesn't change. For parents, though, nesting requires a lot of cooperation and communication, which many divorcing parents find challenging. For some people, sharing physical space, even if they're not there at the same time, feels too difficult emotionally. In addition, it means the adults are constantly in transition, moving between two places to live every few days or weeks.

Nesting can be a good temporary solution if:

- You want to separate but aren't sure about divorce.

- You need more time to think about future finances and housing.

- You're in a financial position where you can keep the marital home and pay for two additional apartments/houses.

- You and your spouse are willing to share two spaces—the marital home with the children and one additional place where you each spend your non-parenting time.

- You and your spouse both have easy, convenient, free places to live when you aren't parenting.

- You and your spouse communicate constructively and peacefully.

Joanne and Francine—Nesting Temporarily

Joanne and Francine decided to separate after fifteen years of marriage. They had five adopted children, including eighteen-year-old twins who would be leaving for college that fall. Selling their five-bedroom house felt premature as they weren't sure how they could afford two houses. They decided to take six months to nest and reevaluate after the twins left for college. They divided up the weeks and created a parenting schedule. Joanne stayed in a friend's guest room on her non-parenting time, and Francine got a studio apartment. Their kids were happy with this arrangement. They loved the one-on-one time with each of their moms and appreciated no longer hearing them argue.

Joanne and Francine, on the other hand, had a hard time adjusting to the arrangement. They continued arguing when the kids weren't around, disagreeing about who should go grocery shopping and mow the lawn, how clean to leave the house, and whether or not they could "stop by" during their non-parenting time. Sharing the house created many of the same problems they had in their marriage. Eventually, the twins went to college and Joanne got a higher-paying job. They negotiated their legal agreement in a way that allowed them each to buy a smaller house. Although they were grateful to have nested in the short term, they were relieved when they each moved into more permanent housing.

If nesting ends up being your best option, follow these five tips for a smooth transition.

1. Create a written document with your ex that you both can refer back to clearly spelling out parenting time and house responsibilities. Who is responsible for the grocery shopping?

The cleaning? The lawn? What are the boundaries for stopping by on non-parenting time?

2. Clarify all housing expenses in advance. If one parent eats steak every night and the other eats rice and beans, who pays for the groceries? What happens if one parent wants a cleaning person and one doesn't?

3. Set up a regular meeting once or twice a week to discuss parenting and house tasks. Consider using a shared calendar to make scheduling easier.

4. Decide on a time frame in advance for your nesting arrangement and meet at regular intervals to discuss how it's going.

5. If this arrangement isn't working for one or more members of the family, it's time to consider other options.

Sometimes nesting works better in theory than in practice. It can seem easy on paper, but the reality of making it work in an ongoing way is much more challenging. Picture this: You are feeling waves of emotion about being separated and show up for your parenting days to an empty fridge, your ex's dirty socks on the kitchen floor, and a receipt in the trash for your favorite restaurant—for two people. Also, you left an important work folder at your apartment and need to go back to get it. You make yourself a cup of tea and sit down to relax but hear your front door open. Your ex forgot their laptop charger and is stopping by to get it. Nesting can be good for kids, but it is often hard on the adults. This is a great example of when "the best interest of the children" may not be in your best interest.

Choosing a Parenting Plan That Works for Everyone

One of the most important decisions you and your co-parent will make during your divorce is how much time your children will spend with each of you. What arrangement would work for you? Your spouse? What is "in the best interest of the children"? How do those intersect?

Ideally, you and your co-parent will share parenting time and decision-making responsibility of your children. Generally, if you're sharing parenting time relatively equally, you'll share decision-making responsibility as well.

In most cases, it's beneficial for both parents to be fully engaged in all aspects of their children's lives. Instead of counting the hours spent with each parent to make sure it's exactly equal, it's preferable to think about how both parents can be involved in their children's academic, social, and extracurricular lives. Ideally, both parents should communicate with doctors, dentists, teachers, and coaches. Of course, this cannot always be the case, but in families where both parents are healthy, functioning, and available, fully engaged time with both parents is generally best for children.

One of the most challenging parts of divorce for parents is adjusting to seeing their children less often. You are facing so much loss already—loss of the marriage, finances, and, for some, your home. Losing time with your children when you're grieving your marriage can be excruciating. It may feel especially unfair if the divorce wasn't your choice or if you're the parent who spent the most time with your children when you were married. What I see in my practice is most women end up enjoying their non-parenting time. It may be hard to believe now, but it won't always feel like torture when your children are with your ex.

On the other hand, being a single parent when your children are with you can also be overwhelming. Doing all the childcare, cooking, cleaning, and emotional labor when you're used to having another adult in the home is a big change. The transition from single-parenting on some days to not seeing your kids on other days can be jarring. It takes time for everyone—adults and children—to settle into a new back-and-forth routine.

Shared Parenting Time Templates

There are many parenting plans you can discuss with your co-parent and the divorce professionals who are working with you. It's important to find a schedule that's in your children's best interest and works for both parents. Ideally, you'll have a co-parenting relationship that allows for flexibility as your children's needs change over time.

Some of the most common schedules are as follows:

Two-Two-Five-Five

One of the most popular equal parenting time schedules is called Two-Two-Five-Five. In this arrangement, the child sleeps at one parent's house Monday and Tuesday nights and the other parent's house Wednesday and Thursday nights. Then they sleep at alternating houses every other weekend (Friday through Sunday nights). That means one week they have two days with one parent and five days with the other, and the next week the reverse.

Pros: It's easy to count on the schedule ("Every Monday and Tuesday you're with me"), and an every-other-weekend schedule works especially well if you don't want to split up your weekends.

Cons: Five days can be a long time for young children to be away from a parent, especially in the beginning.

Hacks:

- Plan an activity with your child during the five-day stretch they're with your co-parent. For example, you have dinner with your children on alternate Saturdays or take them to their swim lessons on alternate Sundays.

- Daily phone calls with your children on your non-parenting time helps to keep a connection during the longer stretches.

- Start with a Three-Four-Four-Three schedule and move to Two-Two-Five-Five when your children (and you) are better adjusted.

Alternating weeks

If you're aiming for equal parenting time, some families with older children adopt a schedule where the child spends every other week with each parent.

Pros: Children maintain connection with both parents. There is less packing, and less transition for the kids and adults. Best for older kids and teens as long as both parents live near their school.

Cons: It can be a long time for a child not to see their other parent. For that reason, this isn't recommended for younger children. Being a single parent for seven days and then not seeing your child for seven days can be intense, making it a hard adjustment for the adults as well.

Hack: Every Wednesday, the children spend dinnertime or overnight with the parent they're not with that week. This allows for a midweek connection without disrupting the schedule.

MON	TUES	WEDS	THURS	FRI	SAT	SUN

Three-Four-Four-Three

On the first week, your children spend three days with you and four days with your co-parent; then, the next week, four days with you and three days with your co-parent.

Pros: Good for younger kids who may find it challenging to be away from either parent for too long. Can be a good schedule if one parent must have weekends but you still want equal time.

Cons: The schedule is slightly different every week, which requires a lot of coordination. Either one parent always has the weekends or the weekends are always split up.

Hack: Incorporate one full weekend a month for each parent.

MON	TUES	WEDS	THURS	FRI	SAT	SUN

If equal parenting time doesn't work...

Please consult a child psychologist and your legal team if you have reason to believe an equal parenting plan will *not* be in your children's best interest. The most common reasons parents would not share parenting equally are:

- A serious mental health diagnosis or addiction that would interfere with parenting safely and consistently

- A criminal record. The courts will determine what is in the child's best interest and take into consideration the nature and severity of the crime as well as how recently it occurred.

- A child's specialized physical or mental health concerns

- A newborn or infant who is nursing; a very young child

- Physical incapacity to parent due to work schedule or military service

- A parent who's been largely absent during the marriage

- Inability to afford a housing arrangement that is suitable for a child

Wednesday/Weekend

If you cannot share equal time with your children, or they are very young, the Wednesday/weekend arrangement may work. With this schedule, a child lives with one parent and sees the other on Wednesday nights and one weekend day, or Wednesday nights and every other weekend. (Wednesday is most common because it falls in the middle of the week, but Tuesday or Thursday could work as well).

Pros: Less transition for the child.

Cons: One parent is doing the bulk of the childcare and the other parent is less involved. The child has less time to build connection with one of their parents.

Hack: The parent who's with their child for less time during the school year has more time during vacations and/or summers.

MON	TUES	WEDS	THURS	FRI	SAT	SUN

Exercise: Create a Parenting Plan That Works

Fill in each of the calendars with one of the parenting schedules above, or a different one you've come up with. Laying out how the weeks will look can help you think through the pros and cons of each option.

Hack: Use two different colors to represent the two houses.

MON	TUES	WEDS	THURS	FRI	SAT	SUN

Your Notes:

Now try making two more schedules. Even if you feel fairly confident you know which one will work for your children, look at a few different options to make sure you develop the one that will work out best.

MON	TUES	WEDS	THURS	FRI	SAT	SUN

Your Notes:

MON	TUES	WEDS	THURS	FRI	SAT	SUN

Your Notes:

Once you have a general sense of the regular weekly schedule, you'll also need to decide about parenting time on holidays, school vacations, and summers. Don't forget about sick days, early-release days, snow days, your children's birthdays, Halloween, Mother's Day, and Father's Day. I highly recommend planning these all out in advance and having them written into your divorce agreement. In the best-case scenario, you follow that schedule but with enough flexibility to make changes as needed. If disagreements arise, you can always revert back to your written agreement.

Once you've decided on a parenting schedule, it's time to put it into practice. There are many ways to support your children as they transition to living in two homes. Communicating the parenting schedule to your kids will be an important, ongoing task. For younger children who can't read, a wall calendar with different colors representing each house can be helpful: "Today is a blue day, which means I pick you up from school, and tomorrow is a yellow day, which means Daddy (or Mama if a two-mom family) picks you up." For older kids, having a calendar in a prominent place in addition to verbal reminders will help keep them organized. It's important for you and your co-parent to plan the schedule in advance, and for you to communicate with each other (not your children) about any changes.

Living in two places and packing every few days or every week isn't easy. It's not impossible and children do adjust, but it can be challenging. Children who are disorganized or have attentional issues may have a particularly hard time. I encourage you to find a packing system that works for your family. Maybe it's a written checklist or a verbal one, a note near the front door, or a text reminder. Your children are doing the hard work of living in two places, so take responsibility for helping them remember what to bring where and when, and try to be patient with them when they forget something at their other house.

Creating a Smoother Transition Day

Transition day is when your children go from one parent's house to the other. The amount of stress involved depends largely on how the adults handle it.

Language matters

If your children have two homes, giving them names other than "Mom's house" and "Dad's house" (or "Mom's house" and "Mama's house") will enhance their sense of belonging to both homes and both parents. Try using a neutral adjective to describe each home. A street name or the color of the house are two good examples.

> Coco and Sean separated when their daughter, Sandy, was twelve. Coco was furious at Sean for leaving and felt frustrated that he was granted equal parenting time even though he hadn't been a present parent when they were together. She was resentful every time Sandy went to her dad's. When Sandy couldn't find her math homework one Saturday, Coco asked if she'd left it at her dad's house. Sandy replied, "Why do you always refer to my house with Dad as 'Dad's house'? You know it's my house, too, right?" Coco thought about

> it for a while and realized her daughter was right. She took a deep breath and said, "You're right. Let's think of a good name for both your houses." Without missing a beat, Sandy replied, "Obviously, we should call them the Blue House and the Yellow House." Coco slipped up a few times, but from then on, she tried to refer to the Blue House and the Yellow House. Sandy appreciated that her mother listened and felt more open to bring up other feelings she had about the divorce.

Don't interrogate or judge

Showing interest in your children's lives is good parenting practice, but interrogating your child about their time with their other parent is not. Keep your interest light and positive rather than asking your child for every detail. Don't make negative comments or pass judgments on your co-parent's parenting time. Children shouldn't feel they're in a loyalty bind. Believing they will hurt one parent if they love the other has a negative psychological impact. Pay attention to your nonverbal communication as well. Eye rolls, deep sighs, and head shaking will only make your children's transition day harder.

> When Amir came back from his father's house on Sundays, he dreaded his mother's questions and commentary. "What did you do? What did you eat? He fed you that? Did you

have screen time? How much? That's too much screen time. What time did you go to bed? He let you stay up that late? You must be exhausted. Was anyone else there? Did you take a shower? I'm surprised he gave you a shower—he always leaves that for me." Amir loved both his parents, but he hated feeling like loving his father made his mother angry. One weekend, an older cousin was visiting and heard the torrent of questions when Amir got home. She was shocked and explained to Amir's mother how detrimental her questioning was for Amir. Amir's mother realized she had to work on letting go of her anger and accepting that she couldn't control her ex's parenting time.

Pick a neutral spot for transition day

If you have an amicable relationship with your co-parent, drop-off can be a good time to update them about how your child is doing. If your co-parenting relationship is tense or hostile, the ideal place for transition is at a neutral location like school or an after-school activity. For example, if your child is with you Monday through Wednesday, it is ideal if you drop off at school on Wednesday and your co-parent picks up from school. This is especially important if your child has difficulty with transitions.

Clara was furious at Archie after they separated due to Archie's affair with his co-worker. Archie moved out of the family home and into an apartment with his new girlfriend. When they first separated, Clara dropped the kids off at Archie's on Saturday mornings. One Saturday, Archie's girlfriend answered the door and Clara screamed at her for being a homewrecker in front of the kids. After that, Archie always answered the door. Clara was so angry that even when she tried to shield her children, she couldn't contain her rage in his presence. The children both complained of headaches and stomachaches on Saturdays, and the younger one started having nightmares. Clara's therapist helped her see that their current routine wasn't good for her children or for the adults. Clara suggested to Archie that he pick the children up from school on Fridays instead, a plan that would reduce conflict between them in front of the kids. Archie thought this was a great idea, and the kids were relieved when Clara told them the new plan.

Dropping off versus picking up

On transition day, it's generally better to drop your kids off than pick them up. For example, if your children are leaving to go to your co-parent's house on Saturday morning, it's best for you to do drop-off. Then, if your child is coming back to you on Sunday night, it's best if your co-parent can drop off. This simple routine helps alleviate stress and anxiety for the kids and the adults. Symbolically, one parent is not *taking* the child away from the other. One parent is *giving* the child to their other parent. It also establishes a routine and simplifies the constant question of who's dropping off or picking up.

> Leslie and Adam had three children when they separated. Their divorce was amicable, and they got along great as co-parents. In the beginning, Adam offered to pick up the children when his parenting time began on Saturday mornings and drop them off Sunday nights. Adam would arrive at the house at the appointed time and stand in the living room as the kids got ready. But inevitably, there were delays as the youngest child wouldn't be able to find his cleats, the middle child would be out walking the dog, and their oldest would be in the middle of an activity. Then there was a round of goodbyes to Leslie with each kid wanting to "get the last hug." Picking the children up became a forty-five-minute ordeal. Finally, Adam suggested that Leslie drop the kids off on transition day. That simple switch made all their lives easier. The kids had some transitional time in the car with Leslie and were not pulled away from her by Adam.

Saying goodbye

Try to avoid telling your child you'll miss them when they go to their other parent's house. This places the focus on you, and they may worry about you or feel guilty. Instead, a simple "I love you and can't wait to see you on Sunday!" sends a message of love and connection.

Lindsey and Reggie divorced when their only child, Devon, was six. Devon spent weekdays with his mother and weekends with his father. When Reggie picked him up on Fridays, his mother always looked sad. "Bye, Devon, I'll miss you so much," she would say. "You can ask Daddy to call me anytime if you miss me, too." Devon liked spending time with his father, but he was an anxious child, and thoughts of his mother raced through his head all weekend. Often, when out with his father having fun, he'd think about his mother home alone and worry she was lonely. Then he'd ask if he could call her to check in. At first, Lindsey loved the calls and kept Devon on the phone for long periods asking him detailed questions about his weekend. Finally, Reggie intervened and told Lindsey their calls had been more disruptive than reassuring for Devon. They decided to set up a quick goodnight call at bedtime, which helped Devon settle into time with his father. Lindsey also realized that even if she felt lonely on the weekend, she needed to use a cheerful tone with her son so he wouldn't worry about her so much.

Setting up two rooms

Your child's bedroom should be a separate, safe, and comfortable place for them to play, relax, and sleep. Ideally, it should reflect who they are—their favorite colors, animals, or sports—and have familiar toys or objects. If you're setting up a new bedroom for your child, ask for their input. Encourage them to bring toys, books, or stuffed animals from their old room to help them settle in. Frame photographs of all the members of their family (including their other parent) to put in their room.

Pack lightly

If finances permit, make sure your child has their own toiletries and other basic supplies at each house, along with an adequate wardrobe. That way, they won't have to pack for every transition. More expensive items like coats and shoes can go back and forth. They may also want to bring special objects with them, like a stuffed animal, to bridge the gap between homes.

It should be the parents' job to transport larger items like sports equipment or musical instruments. Don't ask your child to bring a duffel bag full of clothes to school on their transition day or carry their cello to school unless they have a lesson that day. Inevitably, there will be times you feel annoyed when your child forgets something at their other house. I urge you not to punish or shame them for this, though. Chances are they already feel bad about forgetting their stuff. Your compassion and willingness to retrieve it will make a big difference.

Sharing the Pets

There are a couple of options for how to handle pets after you divorce. In most states, pets are legally considered property—like a lamp or a car—and if there's disagreement about custody, the person who "bought and paid for care of the property" will get the pet in the divorce. Of course, most families consider pets more like family members than property. Some families decide the pets should remain with one parent, while others decide to divide them up. Sometimes families opt to share responsibility for pet care and have them travel back and forth with the children. If you decide to go the route of sharing pet care:

- It's important to consider the needs of the animals as well as the humans. In general, dogs rely on people and are much better at living in two homes, while cats tend to rely on a familiar setting for comfort.

- Make sure you have a clear, signed financial agreement with your co-parent—pet food and vet visits can be expensive.

- Shared custody of a pet can benefit children, but it also creates additional complexity for the adults and should only be considered if your divorce is relatively amicable.

Looking Ahead

Look at all you've accomplished so far! You've Climbed the Mountain and deserve a rest. The work you've done in identifying and processing your emotions will pay off today and into the future. You're well prepared to support your children through their own divorce journey, too. That's a lot of progress!

In Part Three, you'll learn about boundaries—what they are and how to renegotiate them. Creating new boundaries with your ex will be an important step in your healing process. You may find you need to develop new boundaries with your children, friends, family, and colleagues as well. We'll talk about that process step by step.

You'll also read Martina's story. Martina was married to Mickey, who used physical and emotional abuse as well as coercive control tactics to humiliate and manipulate her. You'll learn about how to identify Intimate Partner Violence and coercive control behaviors.

Find a good place to rest, get out your water bottle and snack, and let's turn to Part Three: Recharge, Refresh, Refocus.

Part Three

Recharge, Refresh, Refocus

9

Renegotiating Your Boundaries

It's clear that divorce comes with stress and challenges, along with intense feelings of loss and grief. Yet we also know that divorce offers opportunities for profound growth and change. In my practice, I regularly see women become stronger and more independent over the course of their divorce. Most of them feel more empowered and happier by the end. Nearly all of them renegotiate their boundaries—with their ex, children, loved ones, and themselves—as part of this process. If we think of this period of growth as a cycle that reinforces itself, you can picture how feeling empowered might lead to clearer boundaries, which might lead to feeling stronger and happier, and so on. In unhealthy marriages, the cycle often goes in the opposite direction.

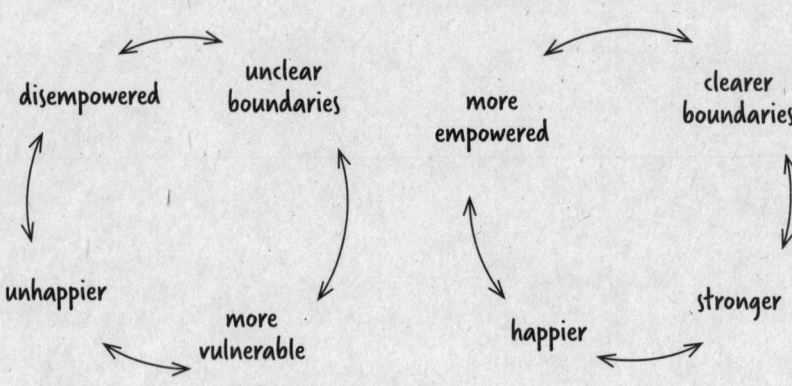

While the topic of boundaries has become popular recently, there's still confusion about exactly what boundaries are. In *The Book of Boundaries*, Melissa Urban defines them as "clear limits you establish around the ways you allow people to engage with you, so that you can keep yourself and your relationships safe and healthy."

In other words, boundaries are not about telling someone else what to do but rather defining what you will and won't accept. They are about *your* behavior, not theirs.

Setting boundaries is an important component of self-care. This includes taking a break when you need one, saying no to things you don't want to do, asking for help, and refusing to clean up other people's messes. You may worry that if you hold a boundary with someone, you will lose them. But in reality, if you don't hold that boundary, you are more likely to lose yourself.

Clear boundaries can help you:

- Strengthen your relationships

- Define your limits and expectations

- Clarify your values

- Avoid overcommitting and burnout

- Enhance your mental health

As women, we are socialized to take care of others' needs, "play nice," and cooperate. These expectations can slowly erode our boundaries. We may come to believe we are selfish or controlling if we set a boundary, and yet it is critical to identify and express our needs. Holding a clear boundary is an essential life skill and a way of respecting ourselves and our relationships.

Good boundaries are especially crucial during a divorce. They help build safety, trust, and respect. You probably assumed that in a divorce, your relationship and boundaries with your spouse would change. What you might not have realized is your relationship and boundaries with other people will change as well. Some of your relationships will strengthen and others will deteriorate, but nearly all will change in some way. Because you can't control other people, this is a good time to focus on your own needs and your role in improving your relationships.

Many women fear holding a boundary will be met with anger, criticism, rejection, or retaliation. There may be circumstances where this is true at first, but that doesn't necessarily mean that giving up those boundaries will lead to a better outcome. If you are a parent, you already know about holding boundaries even in the face of a tantrum. If your child wants cake for breakfast and you say, "We don't have cake for breakfast," they may get upset the first or second time. Eventually, though, they will learn to stop asking. This concept is true of adults as well. If you calmly and clearly reassert a boundary, eventually the person will accept your limit.

Exercise: People Pleaser or Boundary Setter?

Look at each pair of phrases, think about where you are on the continuum, and mark an *X* there. Very few people are 100 percent people pleasers or 100 percent boundary setters, so be thoughtful about where you place yourself. If you lean toward people-pleasing, there will be work to do in setting clear boundaries. If you are already a boundary setter, be sure to use those skills as you navigate your divorce.

After placing yourself on the continuum of each pair, put a check mark next to the statements you want to work on.

People Pleaser		Boundary Setter
Growing up, my family had unhealthy boundaries	_____	Growing up, my family had clear, consistent boundaries
I'm usually the giver in a relationship	_____	There is a balance of give and take in my relationships
I'm uncomfortable stating ground rules	_____	I'm clear about my expectations
I have a hard time saying "no"	_____	I am comfortable saying "no"
I don't like conflict	_____	I let others know when they cross my boundaries
I feel resentful when I do too much for people	_____	I don't agree to things I don't want to do
I say "I'm sorry" a lot	_____	I accept responsibility for my actions, but I don't overapologize
I'm too forgiving	_____	I hold people accountable for their actions

> *You are not required to set yourself on
> fire to keep other people warm.*
>
> **Joan Crawford**

Holding boundaries is hard, but so is giving them up. When you don't set boundaries you may end up feeling a lot of resentment and anxiety. If your boundaries are inconsistent or unclear you may:

- Worry about your safety
- Avoid certain people
- Overcommit yourself
- Receive unsolicited advice
- Dread certain conversations
- Agree to things that are not in your best interest
- Feel anxious about phone calls or emails

Giving up your boundaries communicates that other people's needs are more important than your own.

Three Steps to Make Clear Boundaries

First, you must recognize the need for a boundary.

Use your feelings as a guide. Are you dreading an interaction? Do certain conversations make you feel coerced or insulted? Do you feel resentful about something you've said "yes" to? Once you've tuned in to your feelings and realize you want a change, it's important to get clear on *why* you feel that way.

Example: "I dread every conversation with my ex because he insults me and threatens me about our legal case."

Second, state your boundary clearly.

Find a time when you are feeling calm so your boundary comes across as clear, kind, and respectful of you and the other person. Use a neutral tone and be direct and specific. Remember that other people can't read your mind. Try not to provide a detailed rationale or justify your boundary, as overexplaining can invite argument. It's better to communicate a boundary early on rather than waiting until you you're on the verge of exploding.

Example: "I don't feel respected when we talk. From now on, I will only discuss our legal matters over email."

Third, hold the boundary.

For many women, this is the hardest part. But just like strengthening a muscle, the more you practice, the stronger you get and the easier it becomes. Remember that your limits and needs matter. You are allowed to make your boundaries known and to enforce consequences if they are crossed.

Example: "As I mentioned, I'm moving our discussions to email. I'm going to hang up now. If you have something to discuss, send me an email."

New Boundaries with Your Ex

You and your ex-spouse developed a set of boundaries when you were together. Those boundaries probably included expectations about physical touch, sexual activity, communication, privacy, and access to each other's possessions and finances. Your boundaries likely developed over time as the relationship deepened. In some ways, they became habits. It is now up to both of you to break your old boundary habits and create new ones.

As a reminder, you are in charge of defining and setting your own limits. They may change over time as you learn more about what feels okay and what feels uncomfortable. If your old boundaries benefitted your spouse, you will likely be met with resistance when you begin to change them. Don't give up! While you may choose to keep some boundaries more flexible, it is perfectly acceptable to tell your ex-spouse they are no longer entitled to:

- Engage in sexual activity or sexual communication with you

- Touch your body

- Expect to know how you are doing emotionally

- Expect you will answer nonemergency phone calls, texts, or emails immediately

- Know where you are

- Know who you are with (with some exceptions if you are with your kids)

- Know if, or whom, you are dating

- Know where you work or how much income you make (unless related to child support or alimony)

- Dictate or police your spending

- Have a key to your car or home, or enter your house without an invitation

- Have access to your passwords

- Tell you how to parent your children

- Follow you on social media

Your ex may have their own set of boundaries, which you will need to respect as well. It takes time for both parties to adjust. Have patience with yourself and your ex as you each decide on new limits.

Communication Boundaries

Most divorces involve conflict, so conversations about negotiating a settlement may be hostile, threatening, or just plain unreasonable. The unpleasant tone of these conversations may continue post-divorce if you are co-parenting. You have no obligation to engage with someone who is being demeaning, controlling, or antagonistic toward you. However, being respectful goes both ways—you should monitor your tone as well. A good guideline is to consider what a judge would think if she read your written communications with your ex. What if your phone conversations were recorded and played in court? Would you feel regretful or proud of the way you reacted? When in doubt, keep it as simple, clear, and respectful as possible.

If conversations with your ex become unproductive, you can say:

- "You can't speak to me like that."

- "I'm going to hang up now."

- "This conversation is not productive. Let's continue it at a later date."

- "I'm going to move this conversation to email."

- "I don't want to discuss this further. I'll have my lawyer contact yours to continue the negotiations."

Terry—Learning How to Set New Boundaries

Terry and Scott were married for thirteen years. Scott was controlling and demeaning during their marriage. They frequently got into terrible fights, with Scott hurling insults at Terry until she broke down. Terry finally had enough and decided to leave him. She stayed in their house, and Scott moved into an apartment nearby as they negotiated a settlement. Scott continued to call Terry at all hours of the night, demanding she sell their house immediately or transfer her retirement funds into another account. He demanded to know where she was and who she was with and got angry if she let his call go to voicemail. He came to the house frequently, letting himself in when she wasn't home. Terry was scared of him, and every interaction ended with her feeling confused, overwhelmed, and upset.

Eventually, she joined a divorce support group, where the other members helped her define her limits and create new boundaries. She made a list and checked with her lawyer to make sure all her requests were legal. Then she emailed the list to Scott. All legal negotiations would go through their lawyers from now on. She changed the locks on the house, and he was no longer welcome there. She clarified that it was none of his business where she was or who she was with and that she would not respond to those questions. Scott was initially angry, but Terry kept firm on her boundaries until he realized she meant business.

Terry did a great job setting her boundaries. She tuned in to how she was feeling, realized what needed to change, ensured her limits wouldn't hurt her legal case, and communicated her new boundaries to Scott in a calm, neutral email. She was direct, specific, and clear, recognizing that if she overexplained herself, she would invite argument from Scott. Most importantly, when Scott attempted to cross her boundaries, she held firm to her limits.

Things to Say When You Set a Boundary

No.

No thank you.

I've changed my mind.

I'm going to leave now.

I wish I could, but I can't.

I'm going to hang up now.

Thanks, I'm not interested.

I can't do X, but I could do Y.

I need to end this conversation.

That is not part of our agreement.

My schedule is too busy right now.

I'm not comfortable discussing this further.

I hear you, but I've already made a decision.

I can't take on any additional responsibilities.

Thanks for your concern, but I can handle this.

I can't, but maybe _____ could do that for you.

I'm going to need to think about it and get back to you.

Since we have already agreed to this, I am going to stick with our original plan.

The BIFF Approach: Brief, Informative, Friendly, Firm

If you have a particularly antagonistic relationship with your ex (or anyone else, for that matter), there is an extremely useful communication approach that helps reduce conflict and emotion. I've coached many of my clients in this approach, and with some practice, it becomes second nature. It's remarkable to see how one person can impact a negative dynamic and turn an unproductive communication style into a respectful, reasonable one. This form of communication is especially effective if you are easily provoked by your ex.

BIFF stands for Brief, Informative, Friendly, and Firm. Bill Eddy developed the approach and has written several books on the topic; my favorite is listed in the Resources section at the end of the book. Here's an overview of this approach:

- **Brief:** Keep your communications as brief as possible. Don't react to any negativity—just keep your response focused on the business at hand. There is no need to overexplain or respond to insults.

- **Informative:** Provide information rather than attacks or opinions. Stick to the facts.

- **Friendly:** This one is hard when you are not feeling very friendly, but it goes a long way. Use words like "please" and "thank you" in your response. Keep any negativity out.

- **Firm:** In high-conflict situations, it is best to end the conversation with some resolution as quickly as possible. Therefore, be firm in your response.

As an example, here is a text exchange between Jenny and Mitch. This includes two possible responses, one using **BIFF** and one without.

Mitch: Hey. I am sure you are going to say no, because you LOVE to make my life a living hell. I need to go out of town on Friday, so I need you to take the kids. If you don't, I'll make sure the judge hears about it. You never change, do you? You were selfish then, and you're selfish now.

Here is a response from Jenny *without* using the **BIFF** method:

Jenny: First of all, I don't make your life a living hell. In fact, I made your life a lot better when we were married. Who paid for your student loans? Who cooked for you? I did. Anyway, I can't take the kids on Friday because I have to work late. It's been really busy on Fridays because of all the tourists in town so my boss doesn't like me to leave early, but I can see if maybe someone can change shifts with me. Go ahead and talk to the judge. My lawyer said the judge doesn't even care about stuff like this. I know you think I haven't changed, but actually I have changed a lot. You think I'M selfish???? You're the one who is always cancelling plans with the kids.

Jenny is clearly reacting to a long history of insults and shoots back a few of her own. In trying to defend herself, she overexplains her reasoning. The most likely outcome of this exchange is an unproductive and nasty back-and-forth. Jenny hopes that by defending herself, Mitch will view her differently, but there is little chance of that given their tone. Also, Jenny is leaving the door open to a schedule change by telling Mitch she *might* be able to switch her shift.

Instead, if Jenny uses the **BIFF** method, she keeps her text Brief, Informative, Friendly, and Firm:

> **Jenny:** I got your text requesting a change to the schedule. Unfortunately, I can't make the change this time around. I'll assume you'll find an alternative plan. Thanks.

Do you see how this communication was **Brief**, **Informative**, **Friendly**, and **Firm**? In this case, Jenny keeps her boundaries intact by not overexplaining. Most importantly, she brings an unpleasant text exchange to an end.

It may feel strange at first to be so businesslike, but this is a highly effective communication style for high-conflict couples. Sometimes it can be hard to find the point of the request amid all the offensive barbs. The best response to insults is ignoring them or setting a boundary.

A common question in the divorce support groups I run is "How do I respond to this awful text from my ex?" The first thing I do is empathize with how destabilizing it feels to receive antagonistic texts—it can be overwhelming and trigger painful feelings from the marriage. Then we focus on finding a solution.

I often ask the group member to use their powers of prediction. I might say, "You know your ex best. How do *you* think they will react if you respond this way versus that way? What are the chances they will apologize for their behavior? Will they see your side of things?" If those responses are plausible, then it's okay to explain your reasoning or ask for an apology. But most likely, if your ex sends a nasty message, they aren't going to see your side, apologize, or take responsibility for their own behavior. By defending yourself, hurling back insults, or trying to make your ex take responsibility, you're simply continuing to engage in an unhealthy way. Hitting your head against the wall is not good for you or your relationship with your ex. In exchanges like these, less is more.

Here is another example, this time with Tammy and Roger.

> **Roger:** I bought tickets for the kids to see a baseball game with me this weekend. It's on your parenting time, but you know how much they love baseball. You better not say no, or you will have to tell them yourself that seeing your stupid, redneck family is more fun than a baseball game with their dad who they RARELY see.

Tammy could respond *without* using the **BIFF** method:

> **Tammy:** I can't believe you! You knew we were going to see my mom and how important this weekend is as we are celebrating her 75th birthday. A lot of people are invited and the kids made her a special card. How dare you call us stupid rednecks? Your family members aren't exactly saints. Also, YOU love baseball—the kids don't care about it at all. So typical of you. I wonder why they "rarely" see their dad?? Could it be that he spends all his time with his new girlfriend?? Why don't you take HER to the game?

Tammy's response may be a good way to vent, but it is not an effective way to communicate with her co-parent. Her text also includes insults, and she overexplains her reasoning for holding her limit. She takes a jab at his new relationship, a pain point for her, but one her ex will not sympathize with.

If she were to respond with the **BIFF** method instead, she might say:

> **Tammy:** I'm sorry, but the kids and I already have plans with my

family that can't be changed. You'll have to find a different time to take them.

Using a **BIFF** approach, Tammy responds directly to the demand, ignores the insults, and is Brief, Informative, Friendly, and Firm. Even if Roger responds with another insult, she has already made herself clear and doesn't have to engage further.

The **BIFF** method is hardest to learn for women who were taught to be people pleasers. It takes practice, and even if you use it most of the time, there may be moments when you can't resist firing back a long explanation or list of insults. When this happens, offer yourself grace and compassion, and recommit to using a **BIFF** response the next time around. You will see that the more you practice using it and see its positive impact, the easier it will become.

New Boundaries with Your Friends and Family

Your parents, extended family, and friends will have their own feelings about your marriage, divorce, and ex, so brace yourself for the onslaught. They may also have strong opinions about your legal team, parenting plan, and finances. Occasionally, they may give you advice that seems helpful. Just as likely, though, their advice may feel unwanted, uninformed, or intrusive, even if they mean well. When you find yourself on the receiving end of unwanted questions or advice, it's important to draw a boundary. Here are some things you might say:

- "I'm not comfortable discussing my finances with you."
- "I'm an adult and can make my own decisions."

- "I know you may not understand or agree, but you need to trust that I am doing what is best for me and my kids."

- "It's not okay to talk about my ex in front of my kids."

- "I need you to stop interfering with my parenting."

- "I'd like you to stop inviting my ex to family events."

Of course, once you set a boundary, you'll need to follow through if it gets crossed. That might look like reasserting your boundary or ending the interaction altogether if this happens repeatedly. Here are some examples:

- "I told you yesterday I don't want to discuss my finances. Let's move on to another topic."

- "I know you want to give me advice, but I'm all set. Let's talk about something else."

- "If you continue to tell me I am damaging my kids by leaving, I am going to end our conversation."

- "We are going to end our visit early. We'd love to come back if you can guarantee that next time you won't talk about my ex in front of the children."

- "These are my kids, so I make the decisions about their care. We are going home now. I hope you'll be respectful of my parenting in the future so we can come back."

Vicki—Establishing New Boundaries with Family

Vicki and Shane got married at age twenty. After eight years together and two kids, Shane asked for a divorce. Vicki was very close to her parents and two sisters, who all lived in the same town. Vicki's mother loved Shane and was devastated by the news. She called Vicki daily to tell her how upset she was and to fret about Vicki's children. Vicki was upset, too, and tried to convince Shane to attend marital therapy, but he refused. Vicki's father, on the other hand, was furious and told Vicki she should "take Shane for all he's worth." Vicki really needed their support, but she felt confused and frustrated after they treated her like a child.

When she began dreading visits with them, she knew she had to do something to preserve their relationship. She made a list and told her parents she needed to talk. She opened by telling them how much she loved and appreciated them but continued, "I am going through a really hard time right now. Mom, it doesn't help when you tell me how upset you are. My kids are going to be okay, and I am asking you to stop telling me how worried you are about them. Dad, I know you are angry at Shane, and I am, too, but I am working with my lawyer on getting a fair deal. It doesn't help when you give me legal advice. I want to keep coming over, but in order to do so, I'd like your agreement that these topics are off the table." Her parents were silent for a moment. Then her father started, "We are just trying to help. You are our baby girl and we can't stand

> seeing you hurt." Vicki replied, "I know you want to help, but I'm not your baby girl anymore." Her father looked at her mother. "She's right, you know. We are treating her like she's a child, but she's a grown woman." Her mother looked down. "I'm just so worried about you and the kids." Vicki calmly explained that it was okay for her mother to worry, but she needed to find someone else to talk to. Vicki's father agreed. "We'll do whatever we can to support you. We were trying to be supportive, but I can see how it didn't feel that way."

New Boundaries with Your Children

As a parent, you are familiar with the concepts of rules, limits, expectations, and consequences. Those are all boundaries we establish to give our children the guardrails they need to feel safe. Again, it may be helpful to think of boundaries as less about controlling other people and more about *your* limits. Every parent has their own unique parenting style that considers their children's ages and personalities. While they differ between families, in healthy families, the boundaries are clear and consistent. Consider the following examples:

- "It's not okay to kick me. You need to use your words."

- "I understand you want to stay here, but you need to stick to the schedule and go to your father's this weekend."

- "I can't hear you when you are yelling. When you stop yelling, I will respond."

- "We can talk about it when you are calm."

- "You need to ask before you use my phone. Otherwise that privilege will be taken away."

Once you and your co-parent live separately, boundaries with your children may need to be adjusted. Hopefully, you already have a good foundation of rules and limits, along with consequences if those expectations aren't met. For instance, if you're living in a different neighborhood, you may have new rules about being outside. If you're living with extended family, you may need to talk with your children about your family's boundaries and your own. Inevitably, your finances have changed, and you may need to establish new boundaries around money and spending. Most importantly, there are bound to be a lot of feelings (both yours and your children's), and you should establish clear boundaries about how they are expressed. For instance, your children may be mad or sad about your divorce. Make sure your children know it's okay to talk about their feelings, but acting them out by being destructive or violent is unacceptable.

Lacey—New Boundaries with Her Children

Lacey and Seth divorced after twenty-five years together. They had three children, ages six, eight, and ten. When they sold their family home, Lacey and the kids moved in with her parents while she saved up to buy something new. In their old house, the kids all had their own rooms and a big yard to play in. They played loud music at night and left their stuff around the house. At their grandparents' home,

> however, they had to share a room and abide by new rules about cleanliness. There was a lot to get used to.
>
> Lacey felt guilty about the divorce and wanted to keep her kids' routines the same. But she quickly realized the boundaries she had for the kids in their old house needed to change. At first, the kids resisted her new rules. They wanted to play noisy games at night and leave their belongings around the house like they used to. Meanwhile, her parents wanted to discipline the kids in ways that made Lacey uncomfortable. Lacey needed to renegotiate boundaries with her kids along with boundaries with her parents. One Sunday night, they all sat down to figure out house rules that would work for everyone. It was messy at first, but after a while, everyone settled into their new routine.

Exercise: Setting New Boundaries

Think about your relationships and the boundaries you have with each person. Are there boundaries you would like to change? Make a plan for each one. Remember to set your boundary when you are calm, and be clear, specific, and kind without overexplaining your reasons.

I want to renegotiate boundaries with my ex in this way:
Example: "I need to keep any nonemergency calls between the hours of 9 A.M. and 6 P.M. Please use email if you need to communicate something outside of those hours."

I want to renegotiate boundaries with my extended family in this way:
Example: "I'm building a cooperative co-parenting relationship with my ex. Please don't bash him in my presence anymore."

I want to renegotiate boundaries with my children in this way:
Example: "I understand we've been through a lot of change, but I need you to be respectful when speaking to me."

I want to renegotiate boundaries with my friends in this way:
Example: "I'm not ready to date yet. Please stop trying to set me up. I'll let you know as soon as I'm ready."

I want to renegotiate boundaries with my work (colleagues/boss/clients) in this way:
Example: "From now on, I need to leave right at 5 P.M. to pick up my kids. Please don't schedule any meetings for me that will run past 5 P.M."

Martina's Story

"I had to stay in my marriage to protect my child."

I was nineteen the first time Mickey was violent with me. He was drunk—actually, we both were—and we got in a fight because he wanted to drive us home. We were at a friend's party, and he thought he was fine to drive, but I knew better. When I took the keys away from him, he freaked out. He shoved me up against the car and grabbed the keys so aggressively I thought he broke my hand. I was scared but didn't have any other way to get home, so I left with him. The next day, I had bruises on my ribs and scrapes on my knuckles. He was apologetic and promised to never touch me like that again. Even though I was hurt and angry, I forgave him. I'd never seen that side of him before, and he did seem genuinely apologetic.

He became violent a few more times before we got married, and I always forgave him. He had a really tough childhood, and I knew he was dealing with a lot of trauma from his past. In a way, I could understand why he got so angry. I knew it was wrong that he was rough with me, but I also had this idea that domestic violence meant someone hitting you in the face with their fist. He never hit me, but sometimes he punched holes in the wall. In the heat of an argument, he threw things across the room and broke them. One time when I threatened to leave, he started cleaning his gun at our kitchen table. That scared me. I never knew what kind of mood I'd find him in. After each time he got angry, he would apologize, and I would forgive him.

I spent a lot of time trying to anticipate and prevent angry outbursts.

The problem was that it worked *sometimes*. I'd twist myself into a pretzel, constantly trying to figure out what would make him happy and what would make him angry. Once we were married, he got even meaner, acting like he owned me. Since I wasn't good with money, he took over our finances and put both of our paychecks in his account. He doled out cash to me every week, but it was never enough. I'd always have to beg him for more. He liked being in control like that, but money wasn't the only thing he controlled.

Mickey was jealous and paranoid. He constantly monitored my phone and exploded if I got home late. He accused me of having affairs, questioned my every move, and got upset when I went out.

I started to feel like a prisoner in my own home.

He criticized my friends and family until I finally gave up on attending social events. I was embarrassed by how he treated me when we were out, and it was draining to hear his complaints when we got home. Eventually, I stopped going out altogether.

I became more and more isolated.

I know it sounds crazy, but he always justified his behavior by saying he just wanted me all to himself, and I confused that with loyalty and love. Growing up, my family had a lot of problems, and I wasn't a priority. In fact, they barely noticed me. When Mickey did, I didn't see it as control like I do now. Back then, I saw it as attention.

We had good times, too, but as time went on, the good times were fewer and farther between.

Once we had kids, Mickey wanted me to stop working. He didn't trust anyone to take care of our kids, so I quit my job and handled all the childcare. He wouldn't even let me get a babysitter on the weekend, which meant I ended up with the kids 100 percent of the time. We had really different parenting styles—I thought he was too strict, and he thought I was too soft. He barely paid attention to the kids, and then would have these angry outbursts that left them scared and crying.

When our son was about five, he really wanted to take a ballet class. He loved dressing up, painting his nails, and dancing. This enraged Mickey, who would berate him and tell him to "act like a man." Even on the worst days of my marriage, I knew I couldn't leave. I didn't have a place to go, I didn't have a job, and I sure wasn't going to share custody with a man who looked at our son with such hatred. My kids meant the world to me, and I worried my son wouldn't be safe with Mickey if we got divorced.

I had to stay in my marriage to protect my child.

Mickey was a wheeler and dealer. He owned a few rental properties and a contracting business. He used to brag about cheating the IRS. He wouldn't tell me how much money we had, and I knew his finances were a total mess. There were piles of receipts everywhere in his office, and occasionally one of his clients would threaten to sue him because he'd stopped working on a job.

By the time our kids were in high school, my marriage was hanging on by a thread.

Mickey routinely criticized me and called me fat and ugly. His angry threats and abusive behavior continued. He would trap me in a corner of the kitchen where I couldn't escape, or he'd kick the screen door so hard it came off its hinges. One time, we were coming home from a vacation and the kids were in the back seat of the car. Mickey got upset about something I said, and he started driving faster and faster. He was going ninety-five miles an hour while I was screaming at him to slow down. I thought for sure we were going to die. At the time, I had no idea that kind of behavior counted as abuse. I thought he was just being a jerk.

The final straw came when my son was a senior in high school. He had an adorable boyfriend and they were going to go to prom together. They looked so handsome in their tuxes and rainbow bow ties. Mickey had been demeaning to our son since he was a little kid but had never been violent with him. He got home right when we were taking pictures in the yard and he freaked out. He started screaming, "No son of mine is going to the prom with a guy!" I was humiliated and I know my son was, too. My son's boyfriend started to speak up, and Mickey shoved him so hard he fell and hit his head on the sidewalk. I snapped. That was it. All those years of abuse flooded back.

I may not have been able to defend myself, but I had to defend my child.

I called the police, and after they interviewed us all, they brought Mickey to the station and charged him with assault. The next day, I took the kids and moved in with my sister. I knew divorce was the right thing to do, but it was long and arduous. Mickey hid his money. His paranoia got even worse, and he thought everyone was out to get him. He really knew how to play the victim card. He got a girlfriend right away and paraded her through town, which shouldn't have mattered, but it hurt that he was able to replace me so quickly. The kids had no interest in seeing him, and because of their age, the court didn't make them. I realized I had a lot of healing to do. Mickey was my first and only relationship—I didn't know any different.

Once I got some distance from our marriage, I began to see things more clearly.

It was almost like I was in a fog during my marriage, and when we separated, the fog lifted. I hadn't told anyone about his abuse—

I was too ashamed—but once it was clear we were getting divorced, I started confiding in people. My sister had also been in an abusive marriage (I guess it runs in the family) and her counselor had been helpful, so she gave me her number. I worried the counselor would blame me for staying with Mickey, but she wasn't judgmental at all. She understood that I stayed for so long because I wanted to protect my kids. I didn't realize I deserved better. When I described specific events from my marriage, she helped me to see how they fit into the cycle of abuse. I had no idea that my marriage was considered abusive until I was out of it. I'm not sure where I would be without her help.

It's taken a lot of hard work, but I'm healing now, and the kids are, too. I've been volunteering on a domestic violence hotline, and even though the stories are heartbreaking, it feels good to be giving back. I've been in those women's shoes and want to help them make it to the other side, just like I did.

Can You Relate?

Put a check mark next to the sentences you relate to.

- ☐ I spent a lot of time trying to anticipate and prevent angry outbursts.

- ☐ I started to feel like a prisoner in my own home.

- ☐ I became more and more isolated.

- ☐ We had good times, too, but as time went on, the good times were fewer and farther between.

- ☐ I had to stay in my marriage to protect my child.

☐ By the time our kids were in high school, my marriage was hanging on by a thread.

☐ I may not have been able to defend myself, but I had to defend my child.

☐ Once I got some distance from our marriage, I began to see things more clearly.

> **Oona's Notes**
>
> - In some forms of Intimate Partner Violence (also called Domestic Violence), there is a cycle of abuse that includes increased tension, followed by physical violence, followed by an apology, and then a temporary period of calm until the cycle repeats.
>
> - In addition to physical assault, Intimate Partner Violence includes behaviors that threaten or frighten the survivor.
>
> - Coercive control is a pattern of emotional and physical abuse in which abusers use financial control, humiliation, and intimidation to manipulate their victims.
>
> - Isolating a person from friends and family is another hallmark of coercive control.
>
> - The CDC reports that 41 percent of women have experienced some form of Intimate Partner Violence.

Intimate Partner Violence (also called Domestic Violence) is **aggression or abuse that happens in a romantic relationship** with a current or former spouse, or in a dating relationship.

Intimate Partner Violence can include:

- **Physical violence:** hitting, kicking, shoving, choking, or other types of physical violence

- **Sexual violence:** forcing or attempting to force a partner into unwanted sexual activity

- **Stalking:** repeated and unwanted attention and contact that causes fear or concern

- **Psychological aggression:** using verbal or nonverbal communication to humiliate, intimidate, manipulate, or control

Coercive control is associated with Intimate Partner Violence and is **a pattern of controlling behaviors that create an unequal power dynamic.** These tactics are used to control and manipulate by eroding the person's self-esteem and autonomy. Some women describe their experience of coercive control as feeling like nothing belongs to them anymore: their money, their body, their friends and family, their privacy, and even their thoughts and feelings.

Coercive control can include:

- **Isolating you from friends and family**—often linked to jealousy and control; prevents you from accessing support

- **Monitoring your activity**—always needing to know where you are, who you talk to, and what you do online

- **Asserting power over your body or health**—controlling or demeaning your body, diet, or appearance; controlling your medical appointments; controlling your reproductive choices

- **Denying you freedom and autonomy**—controlling your employment, travel, interests; tracking your movements

- **Name-calling, criticism, and bullying**—behaviors designed to negatively impact your self-esteem, causing you to be more dependent

- **Limiting your access to money**—controlling or hiding finances, prohibiting you from employment

- **Threatening you, your kids, and/or your pets**—used as an additional means of control, especially when other forms of control are no longer working

---

If you've experienced Intimate Partner Violence or Coercive Control, you are not alone. Women from all walks of life have been in your shoes, left their abuser, and created a healthier, happier life for themselves.

If you're still living with your abuser but have decided to leave, the first step is finding a safe distance from that person. Make sure you have a safety plan and a support team to help you leave. Your safety plan is a set of actions that will lower your risk of being hurt by your partner. You can develop it on your own or with help from a Domestic Violence Advocate. Your plan might include:

- Telling a trusted friend or family member about your situation

- Developing a code word with your friend or family member to use if you're in danger

- Writing down important information and phone numbers on a card in case your partner takes or destroys your phone

- Identifying a safe place to go temporarily if you need to leave in a rush

- Changing the passwords to your accounts

- Making sure you have access to your own money

- Documenting the abuse as best you can

Exercise: Domestic Violence True-or-False Quiz

See how much you know about domestic violence by taking this true-false quiz.

1. Domestic violence is only physical. **T / F**

2. Domestic violence only impacts women who live in poverty. **T / F**

3. Once someone leaves an abuser, they're no longer impacted by the abuse. **T / F**

4. Domestic violence can also be perpetrated by women, both in heterosexual and same-sex relationships. **T/F**

5. Drug and alcohol addiction cause domestic violence. **T/F**

1. False. Domestic violence also includes emotional, verbal, sexual, or financial abuse. Some victims of domestic violence are never physically abused. **2. False.** Domestic violence impacts people of all genders and races, people from every socioeconomic status and educational level. The media often portrays domestic violence survivors as impoverished women of color, but domestic violence can impact anyone. **3. False.** The impact of domestic violence can last a long time. People often experience depression, anxiety, and PTSD after leaving their abuser. **4. True.** Domestic violence can be perpetrated by people of all genders and is prevalent in all kinds of relationships, including lesbian relationships. **5. False.** While substance abuse can exacerbate domestic violence, it is not the cause. The underlying issue is often the need for power and control.

FREE & CONFIDENTIAL, 24/7 RESOURCES AND SUPPORT
National Domestic Violence Hotline 1-800-799-SAFE (7233)
Chat online at www.thehotline.org
Text "BEGIN" to 88788

Looking Ahead

You're so close to the top of the mountain now, you can see the summit peeking out from behind the clouds. In this section, you learned all about renegotiating your boundaries. You read Martina's story and learned some additional facts about domestic violence.

In Part Four, Reach the Summit, we'll be reflecting on your divorce journey and the ways it can make you more resilient. In Chapter 10, we'll discuss dating after divorce and how to avoid the most common dating mistakes. Chapter 11 will explore strategies for letting go of anger, how and when to forgive and apologize, and ways of giving back. Finally, you'll find all kinds of mental health, legal, and financial resources, including books, podcasts, websites, and more.

Part Four

Reach the Summit

10

Finding New Partners or Flying Solo

Many women relish the freedom, empowerment, and relief they find after their divorce and are perfectly happy on their own. You may find you don't want a new relationship now or ever, but instead prefer to invest in other areas of your life. Maybe you want to put your energy into your relationships with your children, friends, and family. Perhaps you want to change careers or turbo-charge the one you already have. You might just want to live a calmer, more peaceful life. It's important to choose the path that makes sense in this current moment. Another path may appear in the future, but for now, reflect on what you need in the short term.

Dating Again

Opening yourself up to a new person after you've been hurt takes courage and resilience. It can also be an opportunity for profound healing and growth. Like your marriage and divorce, your dating experience will be uniquely yours. There are no rights and wrongs here—just what works for you.

Dating involves two things—spending time with someone you like *and* doing things you enjoy. I encourage you to date yourself for a while as you heal from your divorce. This allows you to get to know yourself better and be in a healthier frame of mind if you do decide to jump back into the dating pool.

Spend some time relearning what gives you pleasure. You've been focused on other people's needs for so long that you may need time to reflect on what *you* need and want. What activities do you enjoy? What are your hobbies? Are you more of a homebody or an adventurer? Do you prefer cooking at home or going out? Are you drawn to city life or nature on the weekends?

Exercise: Date Yourself First

Perfect Date with Yourself

If you were to spend a whole day **alone** doing the things you love, what would you do? In the spaces below, write down one or more activities you would enjoy in each time period. Be specific!

Breakfast:

_____

_____

_____

Late morning:

_____

_____

_____

Lunchtime:

_____

_____

_____

Early afternoon:

_____

_____

_____

Late afternoon:

_____

_____

_____

Dinnertime:

_____

_____

_____

Early evening:

_____

_____

_____

Late night:

_____

_____

_____

※ ※ ※

Learning to Love Yourself Again

Dating involves doing things you enjoy, but it also involves doing them *with* a person you like or love. When you date yourself, part of your job is rediscovering what you like about you. Being in an unhealthy marriage can take a toll on your self-esteem. This is a good time to get back in touch with those parts of yourself that you like or love. If this is difficult to do, seeing a therapist or attending a support group can help.

Exercise: What Your Friends Say

In the space below, write down at least six positive things your friends would say about you. Are you funny, loyal, or kind? Do you have great hair, legs, or style? Are you loving, responsible, or insightful? Be specific. If you aren't sure, ask them.

1. _____
_____
_____

2. _____
_____
_____

3. _____
_____
_____

4. _____
_____
_____

5. _____
_____
_____

6. _____
_____
_____

    Now that you have this list, put a star next to the ones you agree with. These are the things you like about yourself, too. As time goes on, revisit the list. Add more stars to the things you believe are true and keep building your list.

Dating yourself may feel like enough for you to lead a happy, fulfilled life. Plenty of people do just that. Be sure to continue working on the relationship you have with yourself and your chosen community. Many women are perfectly happy on their own, choosing when they want to be alone and when they want company. If you decide to date yourself, don't forget to buy yourself flowers every once in a while. You deserve them!

You're wiser than your younger self

After dating yourself for a while, you may decide you want to date other people, too. The good news about dating after divorce is you learned a lot from your marriage and divorce—about yourself, your ex, and relationships in general. You're wiser now than when you got married. You may also be looking for a different kind of relationship than your marriage. This is an opportunity to use that learning to your benefit.

Many women face new insecurities about their body being older, wrinklier, and less firm than when they last dated. I have a secret to tell you: Everyone else's body has aged, too. If your date expects you to have a twenty-five-year-old body at fifty-five, that's probably not someone you want to be with.

Exercise: **What You've Learned**

Take some time to reflect on what you've learned about yourself in relationships. Maybe you tend to worry about money and want to be with someone who's financially secure. Perhaps you have trust issues and need to be with someone who gives you a lot of validation. You may have learned you like a lot of alone time in relationships. Write down some of these insights below.

I have learned:

_____

_____

_____

_____

Four Reasons to Wait Before You Date

You may be dreading dating, eagerly looking forward to it, or feeling a combination of both. If you think you're ready to go, be thoughtful about where you are legally and emotionally. There are risks involved in jumping in too quickly. Some people have religious or moral objections to dating before their divorce is final, and others are fine with it. There's no right or wrong here as long as you're honest about your marital status. It really is up to you to decide what feels right. After many years of working with women navigating divorce, I've observed a few main risks of dating too quickly.

1. **You might complicate the legal negotiations of your case.** Some divorces take years to finalize, and you may be emotionally ready long before the legalities are finished. Check with your legal team if you decide to date before you're legally divorced. In some high-conflict divorces, dating could have a

negative impact on your case. I think this is more the exception than the rule, but it's important to consider. This can be true even if your ex is already dating.

2. **Your heart is tender.** This is one of the most important reasons to wait. Dating involves vulnerability and rejection. It can be exhilarating and fun, but it can also be confusing and painful. Your heart is still healing, and you should be gentle with it. If you broke your leg, you wouldn't attempt to run a marathon the day you got your cast off. Treat your heart the same way. It may need some loving rehabilitation before you expose it to any more potential heartbreak.

3. **Your children need your attention.** Your children have gone through the divorce, too, and are doing their own healing. They need your attention right now, and dating takes a lot of energy. Most children also need a period of time when their parents aren't partnered before they get used to them being with someone else. Waiting to date may feel unfair if your ex is already seeing other people, but do the right thing for your kids even if your ex is not.

4. **You may not make good choices.** If you're dating to distract yourself from the pain of the divorce, or because you can't stand being alone, you're less likely to be selective. Dating from a place of desperation or extreme need is risky because you may date the *first* available person rather than the *best* available person. If you have not done enough healing work first, you're more likely to repeat unhealthy relationship patterns.

Cassie—Dating Too Soon

Cassie's marriage was a difficult one. Her husband constantly criticized her weight and her looks. After she gave birth to their first child, he refused to have sex with her anymore, even calling her disgusting. Cassie's self-esteem was so low she worried no one would be interested in her. One day at work, Aidan, a much younger employee, began flirting with her. Eager for distraction from the divorce, Cassie flirted right back. She knew it wasn't a good idea as he was twenty years younger and her employee, but she felt desperate for the attention. She began texting him constantly outside of work and felt devastated if he didn't respond right away. One night, they had sex in the warehouse at work. The next day, everything felt different. Aidan barely spoke to her. Cassie was devastated and tried getting him to talk. Aidan said little other than that he had a "thing for older ladies," and he was sorry if she'd taken their flirtations seriously. Although their time together was brief, Cassie felt heartbroken all over again. That's when she realized she needed more time to heal from her divorce before starting to date again.

A Whole New Dating World

Chances are that today's dating world is vastly different from what it was the last time you were trying to meet someone. Did you grow up meeting potential dates at bars or parties, or from friends of friends? Are you old enough to remember answering personal ads in the newspaper? Welcome to a whole new world. While some people still meet organically, these days the majority meet each other on dating apps.

If this is your first time on a dating site, get your friends to help you choose some up-to-date photos, and think about how you want to describe yourself. Don't be shy about naming your nonnegotiables up front. If you're deathly allergic to cats or could never date a smoker or someone from a different political party, don't be afraid to indicate that in your profile.

Some dating apps allow you to look at their members without making your own profile visible. This may be a good option if you have privacy concerns. Free sites or those that only ask for a picture may attract people who are less serious about dating, whereas sites that require a monthly payment and a written description will generally attract people who are more committed to finding lasting relationships.

There are multiple dating apps out there, so choose one that suits you best. Whether you're straight, lesbian, bisexual, or queer; monogamous or polyamorous; cisgender, trans, or nonbinary; kinky or more conventional; Christian, Jewish, or belong to another faith; older or younger; neurotypical or neurodivergent, there's an app for that. Whether you're looking for a casual hookup with one person or a couple, a long-term relationship or marriage, there's a dating site for that. You can sign up for an app that specializes or a more general one that includes many of the categories above. Before you choose one, reflect on which of your identities are most important to you.

Casual Sex, Relationship, or Marriage?

Many women feel like they go backward in time when they date after divorce, reverting to the age they were when they got married. If you are fifty but got married in your twenties, you may feel like you're in your twenties again when you start to date.

This is the time to think about what kind of dating you'd like to do. Are you looking for casual sex, a long-term relationship, or marriage? Would you like to be monogamous or date a few people at once? It's okay if you aren't sure yet, but keep in mind you'll attract different people based on your preferences.

Some women divorce their husbands because they realize they're attracted to women and want to pursue a relationship with one. On the other hand, some women divorce their wives and decide they want to date men. If you decide to date someone who's not the same gender as your ex, you may need additional support as you find your way. Hopefully your community will be supportive, but some may view this change as a betrayal. Plenty of people have navigated these waters successfully—make sure you find them and ask for guidance. Dating after divorce is the perfect time to tune in to your innate sense of what you want and need and then go for it.

June Confronts Her Sexuality

June and Ben got married in their twenties. June had a relationship with a woman in college that ended right before she met Ben. She loved Ben and the life they built together but always had a nagging feeling something was missing. For her fiftieth birthday, she spent a weekend away with her friends. One night, they all talked about their bucket lists. June told them she couldn't imagine living the rest of her life without another romantic relationship with a woman. Even though she'd had the thought many times, it was the first time she said it aloud. When she got home, she couldn't let the idea go. She found a therapist and talked about what it would mean to continue her marriage with Ben or end it to pursue something unknown. After two years of individual therapy and a year of couples counseling, June decided to end her marriage. Her family and some of her friends were angry with her at first, but many people still supported her. After her divorce, she joined an LGBTQ+ hiking group. Eventually, she fell in love with a woman from the group. As hard as it was to end her marriage, she ended up feeling happier and more fulfilled than she ever had before.

Some women are hesitant to date because they don't want to get married again. It's perfectly fine not to date, but if you do, there are a lot of options available besides marriage. Some women find a partner who likes to travel or go out on Saturday nights, but nothing more. Others want to find a serious partner but have no interest in sharing a home.

"Living apart together" or LAT relationships have gained popularity recently. In this type of relationship, a couple mutually decides to be in a serious committed relationship but not to live in the same home. This can work for long-distance relationships, if one or both partners have children who wouldn't adjust well, or for a variety of other reasons. For more information, check out Vicki Larson's book *LATitude: How You Can Make a Live Apart Together Relationship Work*.

If you know you want to enter a long-term relationship or marry again, take things very slowly. While 42 percent of first marriages end in divorce, the rate increases to 60 to 70 percent for second marriages. That number is even higher if either or both partners have children. People show their best selves first, so take your time really getting to know someone. What are they like when they get sick? When you get sick? How do they react when you have a success? Or a hard day? When your kid has a meltdown? What happens when you disagree? These are all good things to assess over time before you decide to move in together or remarry.

Keep Yourself Safe

Some people on dating sites lie about their age, appearance, accomplishments, and/or their marital status. Knowing this can present a difficult hurdle, especially if your trust was broken in your marriage. Unfortunately, online dating scams are common. Here are just a few things to look out for:

- Their story is inconsistent.

- Their photos seem fake or generated by AI.

- They ask you for inappropriate photos or personal information or send inappropriate photos of themselves.

- They're never available to meet in person or they cancel dates.

- They ask you for money or gift cards—most commonly for medical emergencies or travel to see you.

- Their flattery is excessive before they meet you.

If you encounter any of these behaviors, or anything else that makes you uncomfortable, you can stop communicating and block them if necessary. You don't need to explain your reasons.

Once you do decide to meet someone in person, follow these tips to keep yourself safe:

- **Meet in a well-lit public place.** Make sure you have your own transportation to and from the date.

- **Tell a friend.** Tell a friend where you're going and with whom, and text them when you arrive home safely. If it helps you feel safer, you can share your location on your phone with your friend as well.

- **Stay relatively sober.** You can have a drink or two, but make sure you're in good enough shape to make sound decisions and keep yourself safe.

- **Be clear about your expectations up front.** Are you looking for something casual or potentially more serious? If you're seeking a longer-term relationship, you don't have to have sex on the first date. You've got plenty of time for that.

- **Use safer sex practices.** If you're looking for sex, make sure you take safety precautions. Have you been tested for STIs? Have they? You have every right to ask to see those results. Even then, a clean bill of health isn't a guarantee, as they may have gotten an STI very recently. It's always important to use a form of protection that makes you feel safest.

Five Biggest Dating Mistakes After Divorce

Some women have only dated one or two people in the past, while others have long dating histories. No matter which camp you belong to, keep in mind that it's important to date someone *you like*, rather than focusing solely on whether or not they like you. Don't present yourself as someone you think will be appealing if it means not being your authentic self.

The five biggest mistakes I see women make when it comes to dating are:

1. **Repeating old patterns.** If you date someone who's just like your ex, or reminds you of them, remember that it didn't work out with your ex for a reason. Repeating old relationship patterns is much less likely when you do some of the personal work in this book or with your therapist. If a new relationship feels eerily familiar, pause to reflect on whether this is good for you or not.

2. **Dating the polar opposite of your ex.** Dating someone who is nothing like your ex might mean you swing too far in the opposite direction. Instead of dating someone in reaction to your ex, think about what qualities and values you want in a relationship. Your ex probably had some good qualities, too. They may have been emotionally unavailable, but they were also loyal and steady. Maybe they betrayed you, but you still appreciated their intelligence and focus on being healthy. Beware of dating a carbon copy of your ex, or overcorrecting by choosing someone *completely* different.

3. **Prioritizing chemistry over substance or vice versa.** If you're looking for a casual, short-term relationship, you can prioritize sexual chemistry over everything else. But if you want a relationship that lasts, it's important to have chemistry along

with alignment on other personal qualities. Being great in bed but lousy at honesty, reliability, and responsibility could make for a fun night or two, but you'll need a person with solid character traits if you want a sustainable long-term relationship. Make sure you don't get so blinded by chemistry that you ignore potential red flags. Conversely, someone with a great résumé but no spark is probably not a good fit either.

4. **Dating someone's potential.** Do you have a history of picking fixer-uppers? Do you see potential in everyone? Are you a little too hopeful about people's ability to change? Be careful not to date someone's potential rather than who they actually are. It isn't your job to rehabilitate the world one bad date at a time. Pay close attention not only to what your date *says* but what they *do*. For example, they may tell you they value honesty, but you catch them in a lie early on. They may talk about how important communication is to them and then disappear for days with no warning. While you'll never find someone who's 100 percent perfect, don't settle this time around.

5. **Introducing kids too early.** It takes a long time to get to know someone. Enjoy adult dating without kids being involved for a while. You don't want a situation where you introduce your kids to the person you've just started dating and then break up and restart the same cycle. Take time to get to know your date before doing any introductions.

Exercise: Who Are You Looking For?

Check out the list below and think about the personal qualities of someone you'd like to date. Put a ★ next to your must-haves, a ☺ next to your nice-to-haves, and an ✕ next to any nonstarters. Feel free to add your own ideas to the list as well.

_____ Physically attractive	_____ Intelligent
_____ Sexy	_____ Funny
_____ Sexually compatible	_____ Witty
_____ Similar age to me	_____ Loyal
_____ Much older than me	_____ Handy
_____ Much younger than me	_____ Well educated
_____ Generous	_____ Creative
_____ Thoughtful	_____ Physically active
_____ Open-minded	_____ Has kids
_____ Optimistic	_____ Has no kids
_____ Authentic	_____ Likes kids
_____ Talks about feelings	_____ Wants to have more kids
_____ Insightful	_____ Doesn't want any more kids
_____ Reliable	_____ Likes animals
_____ Proactive	_____ Has pets
_____ Kind	_____ Financially secure

_____ High income

_____ Ambitious

_____ Employed

_____ Hardworking

_____ Lives nearby

_____ Lives far away

_____ Loves to drink

_____ Drinks but not to excess

_____ Does not drink

_____ Does drugs

_____ Doesn't do drugs

_____ Smoker

_____ Nonsmoker

_____ Adventurous

_____ Sporty

_____ Likes to travel

_____ Dislikes travel

_____ Good relationship with their family

_____ Politically aware

_____ Politically aligned

_____ Likes books and movies

_____ Legally divorced or never married

Exercise: What Do You Like to Do on a Date?

A Great Date

Earlier in the chapter, you reflected on your perfect day alone. Now think about the ingredients of a great date with someone you like. Fill out all the sections so you're ready for a breakfast date, an afternoon date, or a dinner date. What kinds of activities would bring you the most pleasure? Be as specific as you can.

Breakfast:

_____

_____

Late morning:

_____

_____

Lunchtime:

_____

_____

Early afternoon:

_____

_____

Late afternoon:

_____

_____

Dinnertime:

_____

_____

Early evening:

_____

_____

Late night:

_____

_____

Ready, Set, Date!

So, your legal case is over or far enough along, your heart is healing, and you're feeling ready to dip your toe in the dating waters. You have your dating app open and you're communicating with someone who seems kind, interesting, and cute! You can feel hope coursing through you for the first time in a while. You may be feeling excited, nervous, and scared all at the same time. I encourage you to keep an open mind. Be selective, but not too picky. In the early days of dating, the only thing you need to decide is whether or not you want to see the person again. You don't have to decide if your parents would approve, whether to move in together, or if you want to get married again. You just need to know if you want to go out one more time.

If you approach dating with the mindset that you will either have a good date or a good story, you may find it more enjoyable.

Try not to spend your first few dates talking endlessly about your kids or your divorce. It's crucial to be honest about being a parent and the status of your divorce, but you don't need to share all the messy details right away. Instead, talk about books and movies you like, your favorite childhood memories, or your hobbies and interests. Ask plenty of questions as you get to know each other.

If you had a sexless marriage, you may either feel eager to have sex again or terrified that you have forgotten how bodies work altogether. This is actually a great opportunity to figure out what you need and want sexually and then communicate those things. Good communication is the foundation of any healthy relationship, so why not start at the very beginning? Remember the boundary exercises you did in Chapter 9? The best time to establish clear boundaries in any relationship is at the very beginning. If your date can't respect your boundaries at the start of your relationship, say goodbye and be thankful you caught that red flag early.

Trusting Again

If you were betrayed sexually, financially, or emotionally during your marriage or divorce, you will likely have trouble trusting again. Being open and vulnerable with new people will be tough, but trusting your own instincts can be even harder. Trust should be given incrementally as the other person earns it, not all at once. It would be foolish to completely trust someone right away, or to never trust anyone again. So be a little bit vulnerable with someone at first and see how they respond. If you feel comfortable with their response, you can open up a little more. Once you have a sense for how they react, and as they open up to you, too, you can increase your vulnerability over time. If you were betrayed in your marriage, communicate those feelings to your date when the time feels right. Let them know how they can help you build trust in this new relationship.

Unfortunately, ghosting has become quite common in the dating world. You may have one, three, or ten great dates and then never hear from the person again. It's hard not to take this personally, but try to see it as a reflection of the ghoster, not you. Be grateful they showed their true colors early on rather than after you'd really bonded.

It feels terrible to be ghosted, so don't do it to people you've met in person. If your only communication has been brief and online, it's okay to stop communications without an explanation. If you meet in person and after a date or two you decide you don't want to continue seeing them, you can send a text rather than make an awkward phone call. Be kind and clear in your communication. Here are a few examples:

- "I enjoyed meeting you, but I don't feel we're a match. Best of luck on your dating journey."

- "Thanks for dinner. I enjoyed our conversation, but I don't feel like we're compatible. I wish you the best."

- "You seem like a great person, but I didn't feel a romantic spark. I'm sure you'll find it with someone else."

If you want to call it off after several dates with someone (and you aren't worried about your safety), talk on the phone or meet in person to end things. Be kind and clear as you state your boundary. If there are safety concerns, a text with a clear boundary is best.

Although I wholeheartedly believe in the healing power of talk therapy, I also believe some wounds need nontherapeutic relationships to fully heal. Therapy can help you identify, understand, and change your patterns, but mutual, loving relationships with your children, friends, family, and romantic partner provide a kind of healing that therapy can't fully replicate. If you decide to pursue romantic love now or in the future, I hope you find it and it finds you. ♥

11

Enjoying the View

> *Who we are in the present includes
> who we were in the past.*
>
> **Mister Rogers**

Here you are, at the end of your divorce. You've got the emotional scrapes, bruises, and scars to prove it. What probably seemed like a never-ending process is behind you. Congratulations for doing all that hard work! You are brave and resilient.

Now you have a new set of choices. Post-divorce, some people sink into denial, hiding their past and pretending nothing happened, while others live a bitter, angry life, letting their divorce define them. But those who've done the work of grieving their marriage and reestablishing their boundaries learn, grow, and heal from the experience. I encourage you to embrace your history and imperfections, as well as the strength that comes from overcoming hardship. You have an opportunity to forge a new identity, keeping the qualities that serve you and shedding those that don't. Your divorce is part of your past, and always will be, but it no longer has to dominate your present. You have the chance to move on.

> *Owning our story and loving ourselves through the process is the bravest thing we'll ever do.*
>
> **Brené Brown**

This chapter is full of exercises that encourage you to reflect on your past, understand your present, and embrace what comes next. These exercises can be revisited in the future as you gain more perspective on your marriage and divorce. I encourage you to do them now, then return to them in six months and a year. You may be surprised to see how much you continue to grow and change over time.

Stronger at the Broken Places

The Japanese Art of Kintsugi

Kintsugi is the ancient Japanese art of mending precious pottery with lacquer and gold. It's not just a way to repair broken objects, but also a philosophy imbued with deep meaning. Flaws are viewed as unique aspects of an object's history that add to its beauty. Instead of discarding the broken pottery or trying to hide the repair, the crack is highlighted with gold. The new repaired piece is considered stronger and more valuable than the original.

Consider your own life. You are a vessel that has been broken in various ways, most recently by your divorce. You were cracked, chipped, maybe even shattered. Now imagine all of those pieces reassembled and mended with a golden lacquer that represents strength and resilience. How will you honor your new imperfect self? What do those gold-filled cracks represent? Can you see the beauty in each one?

The Journey of Sea Glass

A beautiful piece of sea glass you find on the beach likely began as part of a bottle, jar, or vase. At some point, adversity struck, and it became a shard of broken glass. When we encounter broken glass, we see trash and avoid its sharp edges. Yet sea glass makes an incredible journey. Bashed and battered by waves, sun, and storms, it has traveled in the ocean, pulled by the tides back to shore and out again. Over time, its edges soften and become smooth, massaged by the waves and sand. That resilient piece of glass transforms into a tiny treasure to be collected and saved by a lucky beachcomber. Each piece of sea glass is unique and has its own story. You, too, have been on a journey that makes you who you are today—a valuable treasure with a meaningful history.

A broken heart will cure itself no matter how much you wish to keep it broken.

Yoko Ono

Post-Traumatic Growth

Most of the women I see in my practice are relieved when their divorces are over. They're grateful to leave behind uncertainty and conflict. Many of them not only recover and move on but also experience post-traumatic growth. Post-traumatic growth is positive psychological change that can happen after a traumatic event. Research conducted in the 1990s by psychologists Richard Tedeschi and Lawrence Calhoun found that after traumatic events, some people not only survive but thrive. They do this by:

- Recognizing and embracing new opportunities and interests; a willingness to make positive changes

- Strengthening relationships with loved ones and people who've been through similar circumstances; an increase in compassion

- Embracing a sense of inner strength that comes from overcoming hardship; the confidence to handle hard things

- Deepening their appreciation for life; an increased feeling of gratitude

- Evolving or deepening their relationship to religion or spirituality

Integral to post-traumatic growth is the idea that positive change wouldn't have happened without the trauma. While anyone can experience post-traumatic growth, their research indicated it's most common among women.

Exercise: **Post-Traumatic Growth Inventory**

Reflect on your experience so far by answering the following questions:

What new opportunities have you embraced because of your divorce?

_____
_____
_____

Which relationships have grown stronger?

_____
_____
_____

List any new relationships you developed because of your divorce.

_____
_____
_____

List three examples of inner strength that emerged out of your divorce.

_____
_____
_____

What are some things you appreciate now that you didn't appreciate before your divorce?

_____

_____

_____

Has your relationship to religion or spiritualty changed in any way? How?

_____

_____

_____

Reflect on Who You Want to Be

If you have been married for a long time or never lived on your own, it may feel unfamiliar to be living by yourself (or as the only adult in the house if you're a parent). It's now up to you to make your own rules and routines with no one there to support *or* critique you. You can eat what you want, wear what you want, and spend your free time exactly how you want. You get to watch the movies you like, sleep and wake up when you want, and choose how and when to clean your house. This may feel exciting and freeing, scary and daunting, or all those things at once. You have the opportunity to reflect on what you need and desire, along with your likes and dislikes. Most women spend so much time thinking about what other people need and want that they have little time to think about themselves. How do you want to live in the world? Where do you want to spend your energy? How do you want to care for yourself? These are important questions to reflect on as you embark on your new life as a divorced person.

Exercise: Making New Intentions

An intention is a plan that helps you structure how you choose to live. Because many aspects of your life are brand-new, your intentions may change over time. Write down your intentions in the spaces below.

I want to care for myself physically by

_____

_____

_____

I want to care for myself emotionally by

_____

_____

_____

I want to care for myself spiritually by

_____

_____

_____

I want to spend my free time doing

_____

_____

_____

I want my relationship to sex and dating to be

_____

_____

_____

I want my relationship with alcohol/drugs to be

_____

_____

_____

Financially, I want to

_____

_____

_____

As a parent, I want my relationship with my children to be

_____

_____

_____

I want my relationship with my co-parent to be

_____

_____

_____

> *We either make ourselves miserable,*
> *or we make ourselves strong.*
> *The amount of work is the same.*
>
> **Carlos Castaneda**

Five Things to Let Go Of

There are already so many things to let go of during the divorce process, you may be thinking, "Oh no. More?" But letting go gives you freedom, independence, and peace of mind, providing you with energy to focus on your present and future self.

Some people divorce physically, financially, and legally, but never fully divorce emotionally. If you've been reading this book and doing the exercises along the way, you're one of the people doing the emotional work of divorce. This will help with the process of letting go, so keep up the good work!

1. The Narrative

Your truth is your truth and, ultimately, the only one that need matter to you. You aren't going to change other people's stories about your marriage or your divorce, and you'll only frustrate yourself trying. If your ex or anyone else has a different narrative about your marriage or divorce, let it go.

2. Resentment

Nelson Mandela said, "Resentment is like drinking poison and then hoping it will kill your enemies." Holding on to resentment saps *your* energy, not theirs. You've already spent enough time and energy on your ex. When you feel resentment bubbling up about the past, try to release it.

3. Revenge Fantasies

The best revenge is living well. Take back your energy and build something new. If you're experiencing revenge fantasies, you are likely still angry. Take a boxing class, write in your journal, or talk to a therapist. Find ways to express your anger that benefit you rather than consume you. As the Zen proverb goes, "Let go or be dragged."

4. Hope for a Different Outcome

It's time to let go of hope that your ex will change or your divorce will be different. Practice radical acceptance, including mindfulness, relaxation, and positive self-talk. While you don't have to like what happened, you do have to accept it. This is your new reality. The past has passed.

5. Blaming Yourself

It's good practice to take responsibility for how you might have harmed yourself or others, but once that's done, it's time to move on. Repeating a cycle of shame and blame only keeps you stuck. As Brené Brown says, "Talk to yourself like you would to someone you love." Forgive yourself and move forward.

At this point you may be thinking you would love to let these things go, but it's not as easy as just deciding to do so. Actually, part of letting go *is* making the decision to release beliefs that no longer serve you. But there are other tips and tricks that will help you let go, too. Investing in something other than your past and shifting your focus from pain to growth can make a big difference.

Five Ways to Let Go

1. Clear your space

Declutter your home. Get new bedding for yourself. Paint your walls your favorite colors. Throw away or store photos and items that hold painful memories. Make your space truly yours. In addition to your physical space, clear your social media space, too. Block or unfollow any accounts that don't bring you joy.

2. Move your body

Moving your body has many benefits, including releasing endorphins, dopamine, and serotonin, all of which help you feel happier and lighter. Mindful movement like yoga or tai chi can improve your sleep and reduce stress and anxiety. Daily movement improves your mood, physical wellness, and mental health. You don't have to run a marathon or climb a mountain to get the benefit of exercise. Dance in your kitchen after dinner, stretch in the morning for ten minutes, walk up the stairs instead of taking the elevator—incorporate movement into your daily life whenever you can.

3. Change your physical state

If you find yourself drowning in self-pity or rehashing the same negative interaction over and over, *try changing your physical state*. Get up and wash the dishes. Go take a shower. Turn on some music. Walk your dog. Changing your physical state helps change your mental state, too.

4. Help someone else

During your divorce, your mind was consumed with your ex, your finances, your housing, your legal team, and your tasks. Hopefully, there have been people who helped you along the way. Now it's your turn to help others. And, as a side benefit, helping others is a great way to let go of negativity. Need ideas? Leave a huge tip next time you get coffee, help an elderly person cross the street, send a friend a thank-you card, or make a pot of chili to share with your neighbors. Commit to at least one act of kindness per day.

5. Practice gratitude

Keep a gratitude journal beside your bed. Every night, write down three things you're grateful for. Try to be as specific as possible. Cultivating a daily gratitude practice helps you in two ways. First, as you're writing, you appreciate what you already have and reflect on positives from that day. And, in your daily life, you'll be on the lookout for things to add to your journal, improving your mood and overall outlook. Practicing gratitude does not mean that you can't also want more for yourself. You can be grateful for your job *and* want a raise. You can be grateful your home feels cozy *and* wish that it were bigger. You can be grateful your friends are there for you *and* wish they were more available.

Exercise: Gratitude

Make a list of some of the things you're grateful for. Be specific. For example, rather than saying you're grateful for your home, think about what *specifically* about it brings you gratitude. Is it the way the light comes through the kitchen window in the morning or the coziness of your reading nook? Or something else?

Write down what you're grateful for in each of the categories below.

People

_____

_____

Home

_____

_____

Body

_____

_____

Work

_____

_____

_____

Other

_____

_____

_____

Forgiveness

Like boundaries, forgiveness gets talked about a lot but is often misunderstood. When I talk about forgiveness with the women in my practice, many of them react by saying, "Why would I forgive the person who has caused me so much pain?" The reason, I explain, is to release yourself from anger and bitterness. First, it's important to understand what forgiveness is and isn't.

Forgiveness is **not**:

- Denying your feelings of hurt and/or anger
- Approval of what happened
- An excuse for bad behavior
- Permission to repeat the offending behavior

- Forgetting what happened

- Relieving the person of responsibility for their actions

- Reconciling or getting back together

So, what is forgiveness then? First of all, it's a choice. You aren't required to forgive anyone for the harm they have caused you. Forgiveness is a process of coming to terms with the anger and resentment you feel and making the conscious choice to let it go. Sometimes we choose to forgive someone after they apologize and take responsibility for their actions. Other times we decide to forgive without an apology. Forgiveness can free you from your past and help you reclaim your power. It can provide a new perspective and a feeling of peace.

The most important person you can forgive is yourself. Understanding the context in which you harmed yourself or others is an important step in the process. See if you can find a way to make amends to yourself. Commit to learning from this experience and doing it differently next time. Then let it go.

If you decide you want to forgive your ex or someone else who hurt you, you can discuss it with them or keep it to yourself. Forgiveness does not have to involve communication with the person who harmed you.

Be sure you've worked through your emotions *before* you begin the forgiveness process. If you decide to forgive someone who has injured you too quickly, you may deny yourself important feelings of anger or sadness. Depending on how hurt or betrayed you felt, you may decide you aren't ready to forgive now or ever, though I would encourage you not to make predictions about your future self.

Here are four steps to forgiveness:

First, acknowledge how you felt without judging those emotions. Understand the ways those feelings have impacted you.

Second, make a conscious decision to let go of anger, resentment, and bitterness. After all, those emotions are keeping you tied to the person who hurt you.

Third, practice empathy toward the person who hurt you. Empathy does not mean excusing or condoning the behavior but rather understanding the context behind the behavior. Make sure your boundaries with the offending person are clear and consistent so you don't get hurt again.

Last, release any expectations you have of the other person. You can decide whether you want to communicate your forgiveness to them or not. Forgiveness is more about you letting go than forcing the person who hurt you to apologize or change their behavior.

Exercise: **Forgiveness**

Make a list of specific harms you want to forgive. You can pick and choose certain behaviors you want to forgive and others you're not quite ready to address. For example, "I forgive my ex for telling our kids we were getting divorced before I was ready. I'm not ready to forgive my ex for cheating on me yet."

_____

_____

_____

_____

Apologies

Unhealthy marriages and divorces often bring out our worst qualities. It's likely you weren't always your best self during the end of your marriage. That makes sense. Are there things you said or ways you acted that you regret? Are there ways you responded you wish you could take back? If you decide you want to apologize, here are a few things to keep in mind:

- **Acknowledge what you did/said:** "I want to apologize for losing my temper the other day when we talked about closing the credit card account. I cut you off, and I was mean and vindictive. My behavior was uncalled for."

- **Take responsibility:** "I know you were just trying to explain how to close our account. I should have listened before jumping to conclusions, and I shouldn't have insulted you."

- **Acknowledge the impact:** "I'm sure what I said didn't feel good, especially since you were trying to solve the problem."

- **State your future intentions:** "That is not the way I want to communicate. Next time, I will try to listen to what you're saying instead of making assumptions and calling you names."

You can't change the past, but you can take responsibility and apologize for your part in causing harm. You may decide not to apologize now, or ever, and that's okay. At the same time, be careful not to over-apologize or apologize for things that weren't your fault.

Use your powers of prediction when you think about who you want to apologize to. If that person is likely to thank you for your apology or offer their own apology, your actions may be an important step in mending. But if you think the person is likely to use your apology against you or respond by telling you how else you've harmed them, I encourage you to protect yourself by holding on to that apology for now.

Giving Back

The Christmas after I got divorced the second time, I wanted to do something special to acknowledge the many people who'd helped us during that year. I bought thirty paper doves from an Etsy shop, each one the size of my hand. Together, my daughter and I made a list of all the people we could think of who'd supported us that year in both big and small ways. The friends who helped us unpack, the family members who provided comfort, the colleague who brought us homemade chili, the friend who assembled furniture. We wrote each name on a paper bird and strung them together, then hung them up in our living room. We sent photos of the flock of paper birds to every person who had helped us, along with a note of thanks. For me, this ritual was a reminder of the value of community. As a parent, I hoped to model both the importance of asking for help *and* acknowledging those who showed us so much kindness.

After a dozen years leading three weekly support groups for women, I have learned so much from my group members. It has been an honor and a pleasure to see how much women change and grow when they're supported. I'm delighted when I hear from former clients who are still in touch with their fellow group members. Many have become friends for life. These days, most of my referrals come through word of mouth because women who are now on the other side of their divorce reach out to help those just starting out.

I hope you'll take a moment to recognize just how far you've come. You charted your route, packed your supplies, found the right map, and shared your location. You climbed that mountain even though it was rockier and steeper than you imagined. You made it through the twists and turns and found your stride. All the while, you took care of your children, supporting them through uncertainty and transition. You renegotiated your boundaries and learned some of the benefits and risks of dating. Most importantly, you saw how strong and resilient you are and learned more about yourself and your relationships. I hope you feel proud of how much you've accomplished.

Many women feel their divorce was the right decision but still carry a small pocket of sadness nestled next to their heart. Even years after your divorce, when most of your feelings about it are behind you, you may have moments of sadness, anger, or regret. Lean in to your emotions and see what you can learn from them. The next time you're faced with adversity, remember how much strength you gained when you navigated your divorce and call upon it to help you.

You are a member of a club now—the divorced women club—a club you never wanted to be part of. But this club has some of the kindest, wisest people you'll ever meet. Hopefully you found fellow club members who supported you throughout this difficult time.

Now it's your turn. You know what to do. When you encounter someone going through a divorce, reach out, bring food, offer support and resources. Give them this book. Most of all, tell them you understand how hard it is *and* that you know they'll be okay.

Everything will be okay in the end.
If it's not okay, it's not the end.

John Lennon

Ten Practical Things to Do After Your Divorce Is Finalized

1. Update your name and address (if either or both have changed) and remove your ex-spouse's name from official documents and records with various government and financial institutions, including:

    - Bank and other financial institutions, including retirement and investment accounts

    - Utilities

    - Credit card companies

    - Mortgage and homeowners insurance; deed and title to house

    - Driver's license, automobile title, registration and insurance

    - Voting registration

    - Passport

    - Life, health, dental, disability insurance*

    - Post office

    - Social security card

    - Professional licenses

    - Employer

    - IRS, state and local tax agencies

2. Update beneficiaries on your bank accounts, life insurance, investment and retirement accounts.

3. Obtain a copy of your credit score from Experian, Equifax, or TransUnion. You are entitled to one free copy a year.

4. Consult with an estate-planning attorney to help with your estate-planning needs. Update or create your will, HIPAA directives, power of attorney, and healthcare proxy.

5. Obtain a copy of your certified divorce decree. Make extra copies and store them in a secure location.

6. Close any joint accounts, including credit cards, bank accounts, phone plans, and streaming accounts.

7. Review all automatic renewals and auto withdrawal accounts.

8. Update your emergency contact at school/work.

9. Change your passwords on all accounts, including phone, email, social media, and streaming accounts.

10. Create a budget for yourself, and speak to a CPA/tax preparer about your tax-filing status and any changes to filing.

*A special note about health insurance. In some states, you and your spouse can continue to share a health insurance policy post-divorce. You can check with the human resources department of the employer who provides the health insurance or ask your legal team if your plan qualifies. If your ex is the policy holder (also known as the subscriber), you need to tell the insurance company to send your claims and explanation of benefits directly to you. Otherwise, your ex-spouse will receive information about your medical care. Many health insurance companies use a separate company to process mental health claims. If that is the case, you have to make a separate call to that company as well to ensure your privacy. Ask them to send your claims and benefit information directly to you.

Resources

In this final chapter, you'll find lots of resources for yourself and your children. Many of these websites include information and support around multiple aspects of divorce—mental health, law, finances, and parenting—so check them out to see if they're relevant to your needs. Websites change all the time. These are all current as of 2025. For the most up-to-date resources, please visit my website: www.oonametz.com.

Mental Health Resources

National Hotline for Mental Health Crises and Suicide Prevention: www.988lifeline.org; call or text 988 from any phone

Find a therapist on **Psychology Today:** www.psychologytoday.com/us/therapists

Call the member services number on your **health insurance card** and ask for a list of mental health providers near you.

Domestic Violence Resources

National Domestic Violence Hotline: www.thehotline.org; 1-800-799-7233(SAFE); TTY 1-800-787-3224

National Dating Abuse Helpline: www.loveisrespect.org; 1-866-331-9474; TTY 1-866-331-8453; text "loveis" to 22522

Rape, Abuse & Incest National Network Hotline: www.rainn.org; 1-800-656-4673 (HOPE)

LGBTQ+ Hotline—The Network/La Red: 1-800-832-1901

Online Divorce Support Groups

This list includes both free and fee-based groups. Some are time-limited (six or twelve weeks, etc.) and others are drop-in. Check to see if they're peer-led, or led by a life coach, clergy member, or licensed mental health clinician. In addition to offering support groups, many of these organizations provide divorce-related information as well.

Hello Divorce: www.hellodivorce.com

Circles Up: www.circlesup.com

Support Groups: www.supportgroups.com

Woman's Divorce: www.womansdivorce.com

Men's Divorce: www.mensdivorce.com

New Beginnings: www.newbeginningusa.org

Divorce Care: www.divorcecare.org

SAS for Women: www.sasforwomen.com

Rebuilders International: www.rebuilders.net

Rainbows for All Children: www.rainbows.org/resources/divorce-separation

Resources for Finding a Divorce Professional

Avvo: www.avvo.com Online directory to find an attorney of any kind, including divorce.

American Academy of Matrimonial Lawyers: www.aaml.org Online directory to find a divorce attorney.

Academy of Professional Family Mediators: www.apfmnet.org Online directory to find a mediator.

JAMS Mediation, Arbitration, and ADR Services: www.jamsadr.com Online directory to find a mediator (called "Neutrals" on this site).

Amicable Divorce Network: www.amicabledivorcenetwork.com Online directory to find a wide range of divorce professionals in the fields of law, mediation, mental health, and finance.

Fresh Starts: www.freshstartsregistry.com Started by two sisters, this is one of my favorite websites. In addition to their divorce registry, they have a directory of divorce experts, a podcast, and a wealth of free information on their website.

Divorce Net: www.divorcenet.com Information, quizzes, and resources for filing for divorce online without an attorney.

Vesta Divorce: www.vestadivorce.com Online directory of divorce professionals as well as free webinars and events.

Free or Low-Cost Legal Services

National Association of Community Mediation: www.nafcm.org

Law Help: www.lawhelp.org

LGBTQ+ Bar: www.lgbtqbar.org

Financial Resources

Marriage is About Love, Divorce is About Money: The Business of Divorce by Gabrielle Clemens, JD, LLM, AEP, CDFA This is a user-friendly step-by-step guide to the legal and financial process of divorce from an attorney and Certified Divorce Financial Analyst.

The Institute for Divorce Financial Analysts: www.institutedfa.com Online directory to find a Certified Divorce Financial Analyst.

Association of Divorce Financial Planners: www.divorceandfinance.org Online directory to find a Certified Divorce Financial Analyst.

Free Credit Report: www.annualcreditreport.com Be sure to get a free credit report once a year, especially when you're going through a divorce.

Federal benefits: www.usa.gov/benefit-finder Check this website to see if you're eligible for any federal benefits.

Recommended Books

Trauma and Recovery

When Things Fall Apart by Pema Chödrön

Keep Moving by Maggie Smith

Journey Through Trauma by Gretchen Schmelzer

Trauma and Recovery by Judith Herman

Daring Greatly by Brené Brown

Rising Strong by Brené Brown

More Recommended Books

Infidelity

After the Affair: Healing the Pain and Rebuilding Trust When a Partner Has Been Unfaithful by Janis Spring

The State of Affairs: Rethinking Infidelity by Esther Perel

Leave a Cheater, Gain a Life: The Chump Lady's Survival Guide by Tracy Schorn

Runaway Husbands: The Abandoned Wife's Guide to Recovery and Renewal by Vikki Stark

Narcissism

It's Not You: Identifying and Healing from Narcissistic People by Ramani Durvasula, PhD

Rethinking Narcissism: The Secret to Recognizing and Coping with Narcissists by Dr. Craig Malkin

Effective Co-Parenting or Parallel Parenting with a Narcissist by Claire Brown

Disarming the Narcissist: Surviving and Thriving with the Self-Absorbed by Wendy Behary

Boundaries

Set Boundaries, Find Peace by Nedra Tawwab

Real Self-Care: A Transformative Program for Redefining Wellness by Pooja Lakshmin

The Book of Boundaries by Melissa Urban

Divorce Memoirs

This American Ex-Wife by Lyz Lenz

Splinters by Leslie Jamison

You Could Make This Place Beautiful by Maggie Smith

Untamed by Glennon Doyle

This Story Will Change by Elizabeth Crane

The Leaving Season by Kelly McMasters

Blow Your House Down by Gina Frangello

Heartbreak: A Personal and Scientific Journey by Florence Williams

Podcasts

We Can Do Hard Things with Glennon Doyle, Abby Wambach, and Amanda Doyle

A Fresh Story and *Divorce Happens* with Olivia Dreizen and Jenny Dreizen

The Rewrite with Wendy Sloane

D Shift with Mardi Winder-Adams

Divorce and Beyond with Susan Guthrie

The Divorce Survival Guide with Kate Anthony

Divorced Girl Smiling with Jackie Pilossoph

Co-Parenting Resources

Co-Parenting Apps

If you have a high-conflict divorce, an unreliable co-parent, or you just want to streamline your communications, these apps are designed specifically for co-parents. Support with communication, scheduling, and shared expenses.

Our Family Wizard: www.ourfamilywizard.com

Talking Parents: www.talkingparents.com

App Close: www.appclose.com

Co-Parenting Books

BIFF for CoParent Communication: Your Guide to Difficult Texts, Emails, and Social Media Posts by Bill Eddy, Annette Burns, and Kevin Chafin

Cooperative Co-Parenting for Secure Kids: The Attachment Theory Guide to Raising Kids in Two Homes by Aurisha Smolarski

The Co-Parenting Handbook: Raising Well-Adjusted and Resilient Kids from Little Ones to Young Adults through Divorce or Separation by Karen Bonnell with Kristin Little

Combative to Collaborative: The Co-Parenting Code by Teresa Harlow

Surviving and Thriving in Stepfamily Relationships by Patricia Papernow

The Stepfamily Handbook by Karen Bonnell and Patricia Papernow

Children's Books on Divorce and Stepfamilies

Why Do Families Change? by Dr. Jillian Roberts

Always Mom, Forever Dad by Joanna Rowland

Living with Mom and Living with Dad by Melanie Walsh

Here and There by Tamara Ellis Smith

Weekend Dad by Naseem Hrab

You Make Your Parents Super Happy! A Book About Parents Separating by Richy Chandler

Room for Rabbit by Roni Schotter

Getting Used to Harry by Cari Best

Acknowledgments

I am so grateful to all the people who have helped these pages become a book. The members of my support groups show up every week with honesty, vulnerability, and courage, and without them, this book would not exist. To all my clients who have navigated divorce—thank you for sharing your stories with me. It is a great honor and a privilege to hear them. I hope our time together helped you heal, and I know the experiences you shared will help other women navigating divorce for years to come.

I could not have written this book without the wise, attuned, laser-sharp counsel of Katie Bannon. Writing coach, editor, cheerleader extraordinaire—she climbed this mountain with me every step of the way, and I will forever be grateful. Katie—you gave me a map, showed me the way, pushed me when the going was tough, and provided nourishment and reassurance until we made it to the top. Thank you from the bottom of my heart.

There were so many readers of these pages who added commas and comments, ideas and encouragement, and I am thankful to them all: Amy R, Susan M, Lisa G, Lisa C, Craig, Erin, Kate F, Ben, Marcia, Liz

M, Siobhan, Mosie, Theresa, my dad and Cleopatra, Marisa, Richard, Gabrielle, Heidi, Julie, Jen V, Patricia, Sharon, Steve, Suzanne, Vicki, Margaret, Sherry, Sarah, and Eliot. Barb, Amy, Joyce, Christine, and Kelley—you were the best cheerleaders. And to Luke, thanks for the title ideas.

My writing group was immensely helpful and read early drafts of chapters with grace and wisdom. Thank you, Tanya, Christie, and Meg. I love our Tuesdays together.

Thank you to my co-parents—we raised some awesome kids.

I wrote this book in my head, on my couch in Massachusetts, in the mountains of Vermont, on vacation in Mexico, on a porch in Martha's Vineyard, and at an Airbnb in Boulder. The idea sprang from my head on a mountaintop on a friend's fifty-fifth birthday hike. Thanks for the hike and inspiration, Annie!

My agent Mel Flashman and the folks at Janklow & Nesbit have been wonderful to work with. Thank you, Luke Janklow, Mel Flashman, and Jess Gitre, for believing in me and this project. My editor, Pamela Cannon, and the Gallery Books team of Hanna Preston, Jill Siegel, Emma Skeels, and Karla Schweer have been invaluable. I am grateful for the opportunity to work with this talented group. Thank you all.

My family was encouraging and patient, and my kids cheered me on from the very beginning. To my kids—you light up my life and make everything better. Thank you.

An especially big thank-you to Lynda, who believed in me, cheered me on, took care of nearly everything while I wrote, and endured countless read-aloud sessions on the couch. Lynda, you are indeed "the best one."

Endnotes

Introduction

p. 10 **According to a study from the University of Michigan . . .**

Laurel Thomas, "Exactly How Much Housework Does a Husband Create?" U Michigan News, April 3, 2008, https://news.umich.edu/exactly-how-much-housework-does-a-husband-create.

p. 10 **Research shows that marriage benefits men . . .**

Daniel A. Cox, "Is Marriage Better for Men?" Survey Center on American Life, November 30, 2023, https://www.americansurveycenter.org/newsletter/is-marriage-better-for-men/.

Joan Monin and Margaret Clark, "Why Do Men *Benefit* More from Marriage Than Do Women? Thinking More Broadly about Interpersonal Processes That Occur Within *and* Outside of Marriage," *Sex Roles: A Journal of Research* 65, no. 5–6 (2011): 320–26.

"Marriage and Men's Health," Harvard Health Publishing, June 5, 2019, https://www.health.harvard.edu/mens-health/marriage-and-mens-health.

p. 11 **In the US, heterosexual women initiate 69 percent of divorces . . .**

Michael Rosenfeld, "Who Wants the Breakup? Gender and Breakup in Heterosexual Couples," American Sociological Association 110th Annual Meeting, August 22–25, 2015.

p. 12 **In fact, data from the Bureau of Labor Statistics . . .**

Joanna Pepin, Liana Sayer, and Lynne Casper, "Marital Status and Mothers' Time Use: Childcare, Housework, Leisure, and Sleep," *Demography* 55, no. 1 (2018): 107–33.

Chapter 1: Getting Oriented

p. 36 **A somatic release helps regulate . . .**

Francesca Krempa, "This Easy 'Somatic Release' Exercise Helps You Destress in 60 Seconds Flat," *Well + Good*, June 30, 2021, https://www.wellandgood.com/health/somatic-release-exercise.

Chapter 2: Preparing for Your Journey

p. 60 **In her book** *Real Self-Care* **. . .**

Pooja Lakshmin, MD, *Real Self-Care: A Transformative Program for Redefining Wellness* (Penguin Life, 2023), xx.

p. 71 **However, much of the current research . . .**

Alexandrea L. Craft, Maureen Perry-Jenkins, and Katie Newkirk, "The Implications of Early Marital Conflict for Children's Development," *Journal of Child and Family Studies* 30, no. 1 (2021): 292–310.

Margaret's Story

p. 82 **Lesbians marry and divorce . . .**

Carmela DeNicola, "LGBTQ Couples and Divorce Trends," Mediate.com, July 5, 2022, https://mediate.com/lgbtq-couples-and-divorce-trends/.

Chapter 3: Following the Map

p. 86 **Elisabeth Kübler-Ross developed . . .**

Elisabeth Kübler-Ross and David Kessler, *On Grief and Grieving: Finding the Meaning of Grief Through the Five Stages of Loss* (Scribner, 2005).

Mandy's Story

p. 100 **Narcissistic Personality Disorder, or NPD . . .**

American Psychiatric Association, *Diagnostic and Statistical Manual of Mental Disorders, Fifth Edition, Text Revision* (American Psychiatric Publishing, 2022).

p. 101 **The narcissistic abuse cycle . . .**

Ramani Durvasula, *It's Not You: Identifying and Healing from Narcissistic People* (Open Field, 2024).

p. 103 **Many narcissists are reluctant . . .**

Craig Malkin, *Rethinking Narcissism: The Secret to Recognizing and Coping with Narcissists* (Harper Perennial, 2016).

Chapter 5: Staying on the Trail

p. 129 **There's a wonderful children's book . . .**

Michael Rosen and Helen Oxenbury, *We're Going on a Bear Hunt* (Walker Books, 2015).

p. 142 **The Holmes-Rahe Stress Scale . . .**

Peter A. Noone, "The Holmes–Rahe Stress Inventory," *Occupational Medicine* 67, no. 7 (2017): 581–82.

Chapter 6: Hitting Your Stride

p. 167 **. . . humming can promote multiple mental and physical health benefits . . .**

Gunjan Trivedi, Kamal Sharma, Banshi Saboo, et al., "Humming (Simple Bhramari Pranayama) as a Stress Buster: A Holter-Based Study to Analyze Heart Rate Variability (HRV) Parameters During Bhramari, Physical Activity, Emotional Stress, and Sleep," *Cureus* 15, no. 4 (2023).

Chapter 7: Preparing Children for the Journey Ahead

p. 188 **Stigma about divorce and its impact . . .**

Julia Lewis, Sandra Blakeslee, and Judith Wallerstein, *The Unexpected Legacy of Divorce: The 25 Year Landmark Study* (Hyperion, 2000).

p. 188 **However, over the next two decades . . .**

Joan Kelly and Robert Emery, "Children's Adjustment Following Divorce: Risk and Resilience Perspectives," *Family Relations: An Interdisciplinary Journal of Applied Family Studies* 52, no. 4 (2003): 352–362.

p. 189 **A 2013 *Scientific American* article . . .**

Hal Arkowitz and Scott O. Lilienfeld, "Is Divorce Bad for Children?" *Scientific American*, March 2013, https://www.scientificamerican.com/article/is-divorce-bad-for-children/.

p. 189 **In fact, many studies . . .**

Rebecca Brock and Grazyna Kochanska, "Interparental Conflict, Children's Security with Parents, and Long-Term Risk of Internalizing Problems: A Longitudinal Study from Ages 2 to 10," *Development and Psychopathology* 28, no. 1 (2016): 45-54.

p. 189 **It's also clear that parents . . .**

Marta Herrero, Ana Martínez-Pampliega, and Irati Alvarez, "Family Communication, Adaptation to Divorce and Children's Maladjustment: The Moderating Role of Co-parenting," *Journal of Family Communication* 20, no. 2 (2020): 114–128.

p. 202 **I want to reassure you . . .**

Rebecca Ryan, Anne Martin, and Jeanne Brooks-Gunn, "Is One Good Parent Good Enough? Patterns of Mother and Father Parenting and Child Cognitive Outcomes at 24 and 36 Months," *Parenting: Science and Practice* 6, no. 2–3 (2006): 211–28.

Chapter 9: Renegotiating Your Boundaries

p. 238 **In *The Book of Boundaries* . . .**

Melissa Urban, *The Book of Boundaries: Set the Limits That Will Set You Free* (Dial Press, 2023), 6.

p. 248 **Here's an overview . . .**

Bill Eddy, Annette Burns, and Kevin Chafin, *BIFF for CoParent Communication: Your Guide to Difficult Texts, Emails, and Social Media Posts* (Unhooked Books, 2020).

Martina's Story

p. 265 **Coercive control is associated . . .**

Lisa Aronson Fontes, *Invisible Chains: Overcoming Coercive Control in Your Intimate Relationship* (Guilford Press, 2015).

Chapter 11: Enjoying the View

p. 300 **Research conducted in the 1990s . . .**

Richard Tedeschi and Lawrence Calhoun, "The Posttraumatic Growth Inventory: Measuring the Positive Legacy of Trauma," *Journal of Traumatic Stress* 9, no. 3 (1996): 455–71.

About the Author

Oona Metz is a therapist and author who lives in Massachusetts with her partner and a handful of pets. Her children have flown the coop, but return home often. Her greatest joy in life so far has been being a mother and stepmother.